Hospice in the Hood
During the Ferguson, Missouri, Riots

By Tia Rees

Hospice in the Hood

Copyright ©2016 by Tia Rees

All Rights Reserved

No part of this publication may be reproduced, stored in a retrieval system, or transmitted, in any form or by any means, electronic, mechanical, photocopying, recording, or otherwise, without the written permission of the author.

First published by Dog Ear Publishing
4011 Vincennes Rd
Indianapolis, IN 46268
www.dogearpublishing.net

ISBN: 978-1-4575-4705-8

This book is printed on acid-free paper.

Printed in the United States of America

Disclaimer from the Author
This book is based on the real-life stories of my patients and their families. In order to respect their privacy, however, every attempt has been made to conceal their identities. No one is identified by name, family member names, friends' names, exact age, place of residence, most physical descriptions, street names, number and gender of family members, what disease they have, patients' medications and treatment plan, and where they work or their profession, including my place of employment. The only exceptions include, but are not limited to the security personnel who agreed to be identified and granted legal permission.

Dedication

Many thanks to my father, mother and friends who encouraged me to write down these life-changing stories and events. Thanks also to my editor, Ellen, who worked to refine the manuscript, and to Stevie Wonder, whose amazing music is occasionally referred to in this book.

The stories in this book are dedicated to all of my fellow hospice colleagues who provide a very special kind of healing at the end of an individual's life. They are nurses, social workers, chaplains, doctors, nurse practitioners, supervisors, medical directors, pharmacists, counselors, home health aides, volunteers, and my security personnel, John, Tom and Patrick. And most important, to my dying patients and their families and to all those who passed as I was taking care of them—and as they, in turn, were looking out for me. See you in heaven.

"If a soul is left in the darkness, sins will be committed.
The guilty one is not he who commits the sin,
but the one who causes the darkness."

—*Victor Hugo*

Foreword

In each person's life there comes a pivotal point, event or period of time. During this period of time an individual can experience "high highs" and "low lows," along with very short intervals of "just another ordinary day." During these times, so much happens so quickly, often with no frame of reference to process the events. There is no "down time" to reflect. There is only time to react. These meaningful, eventful or dramatic periods change our lives—sometimes for the better and sometimes for the worse.

For some individuals, these periods of dramatic life change occur as they serve our country. For others, their lives are changed by a major athletic achievement or crushing sports failure. Some have their lives altered irrevocably by going to prison, overcoming addiction, or having a near-death experience. In any case, the person is never the same.

It is my belief that the three years of experiences written about in the pages of this book represent that life-changing turning point for the author, Tia Rees. While she is still relatively young, she will probably never again be in a position to witness and participate in a similar confluence of life events. Tia's responsibility is to take care of dying patients and their families—a unique vocation that can only be done by very special people—and they are out there. Most would say that such a job would be extremely difficult in a safe environment, but Tia, a young white woman, served primarily African-American communities hit hard by poverty, violence and crime. She did so during the unsafe and dramatic conditions that resulted from the Michael Brown shooting and the subsequent riots, unrest and racial tension of 2014.

Tia's reality, as she described it to me, was that she loved what she was doing because of the appreciation shown to her on a daily basis from her patients and their families. That is what motivated her. She knows there are others who go out and do exactly what she does. She knows she is not special in that respect.

This book is a collection of stories from her experiences. None of the stories are alike.

In the conversations I have had with her over the past three years, the most interesting stories and topics included really funny things that happened with her patients and families and the great conversations they were able to have about race.

Tia notes that there was as much laughing as crying—and both happened on most days. When people are dying, they and their families normally "cut to the chase" in conversations. There isn't time for pettiness or distractions. The result is that they can be honest and candid and share entirely genuine points of view. In these days of racial tension and misunderstanding, perhaps the end-of-life setting, however unfortunate, allows individuals to better relate to one another not as black or white, but simply as human beings, with all of their pain, frustration, fear and vulnerability laid bare.

Under such conditions, relationships form "lightning fast.". There is no time for delicately dancing around issues. The result of this was that every day on the job Tia was able to get close to many people on a very deep level.

Readers who don't know much about "hospice," will learn about the community-based services provided by hospice caregivers when a person comes to the end of life and wants to be cared for at home. Also readers will read intimate details of Tia's experiences as she went about her daily business in dealing with patients and their families.

Tia has a big personality but is a humble person when she talks about what she does. She knows that many others do more difficult work, whether in this country or beyond. But for Tia, her nursing experiences over the past three years were a big deal and certainly the most interesting thing she ever accomplished.

Tia also faced the grim reality that she did not see a great deal of hope in the eyes of the people she got to know—and they rarely expressed any. This changed and saddened her. She did, however, meet and become friends with many wonderful individuals and interesting characters, and she remains in contact with several family members to this day.

Tia wrote this book for two reasons. She believes she may have experienced some situations that others will find as interesting, as sad, as funny, and as weird as she did, and she thinks they will enjoy reading about them. She also wanted to document and record the end-of-life journeys of some of the great people she had the honor to come to know—and now you will also meet them in this book. They will live forever in the pages of this book. Tia thinks they deserve this, and she hopes you will think so, too.

Tom Rees

Table of Contents

Chapter 1	Shots Fired, Bring-Your-Dad-to-Work Day	1
Chapter 2	Little Red Riding Hood in the Hood	6
Chapter 3	John Riggins, Soccer and Gommie	9
Chapter 4	Neighborhood Watch-Out	12
Chapter 5	The Man Who Takes Lollipops from the Bank	14
Chapter 6	Curb Service Hospice	22
Chapter 7	My Audition for a Job	28
Chapter 8	Ted and Tia for President	36
Chapter 9	Yes, You in the Backyard, Come Out and Answer Your Door!	45
Chapter 10	My Dad Doesn't Believe in Heaven, so There!	49
Chapter 11	I Took My Dying Dad's Pills for My Toothache	53
Chapter 12	How Many Accountants Does It Take to Give a Dying Patient Her Meds?	55
Chapter 13	I Hate White People	58
Chapter 14	Nature Calls	67
Chapter 15	August 2014: The Whole World Watches as Ferguson, Missouri, Erupts	72
Chapter 16	Murder and Baseball	82
Chapter 17	They Can Kiss My Black Ass	86
Chapter 18	Buddy and Drug Business—But Not on My Watch	91
Chapter 19	The Coffin in the White Folks' Front Yard	95
Chapter 20	They Are Just Babies, for God's Sake!	98
Chapter 21	Stag Beer, Vanilla Ice Cream and Death	102
Chapter 22	Sometimes You May Not Want a Medical Person to Take Care of You	109

Chapter 23	"F" Those People	114
Chapter 24	The Hospice Dating Scene	120
Chapter 25	I Smell Gas and It Is Not Coming from a Patient	125
Chapter 26	White People Have a Different Rule	131
Chapter 27	Ferguson Burns	137
Chapter 28	Two Weeks of Hell	141
Chapter 29	The Flames Spread from Ferguson	145
Chapter 30	Christmas and Hospice	149
Chapter 31	Missouri: Murder Capital of the U.S.	157
Chapter 32	The Best Days of My Life	160
Appendix I	About Hospice	163

CHAPTER 1

Shots Fired, Bring-Your-Dad-to-Work Day

One evening I was in East St Louis, Illinois. It was about eight in the evening and seemed especially dark. This was a very rough area—the houses that still remained were old and very run down. Abandoned houses sat next door to and across from the home I was to visit. Next to these were several empty lots strewn with trash and overgrown with weeds that had grown so high they had fallen over. There were no street signs—only bent-over poles where signs had once hung. The neighborhood did not seem to have any streetlights, but dim lights and the soft red electric glow of space heaters radiated from the homes that were occupied. It was really cold outside; the wind swirled a dusting of snow around on the frozen ground.

I arrived at the home and there were cars parked everywhere, including in the front yard. I glanced in the back yard and saw two pit bulls running through the legs of the people in the yard. There were thirty or so African Americans, mostly men, outside. They were talking, drinking beer, and engaging in lively conversations.

I was a little shook up. I'd had a hard time finding my way to the police station to get an officer to follow me to the home. MapQuest doesn't work well when there are few street signs, and there were barricades on every other street. I realized

I seemed out of place. I am a young woman and very white. I looked through the gathering in the back yard and saw one other white person there. He was a small, kind of skinny man, but he appeared to be fitting in nicely with the group.

This is my job and I love it.

I was there as a hospice nurse to officially pronounce the passing of one of my patients and to take care of all the needs of the family. I had been a traveling nurse for over fifteen years and worked in hospitals all over the country. I had worked in many places including San Francisco, Phoenix, South Carolina, Burbank, St. Louis, and most recently, Las Vegas.

I had wanted a change and I got it. I returned home and looked for a job in hospice care. This was the first hospice job I'd ever had. Most of my visits until this point had been in rural areas but some were in the East St. Louis area.

About a week before, I had made one other house call in this area and shared my experience with my boss and my family. We decided that it was unsafe for me to go into the area without some assistance. My boss suggested that we request police escort because they had offered to go with us in the past. My boss also noted that the ambulances going into the area are always accompanied by the police.

I called the police and they told me they had no problem with accompanying me. In fact, they thought that this was a good idea. So when I received the assignment, I called them, and they instructed me to meet them at the police station so that we would be good to go.

I felt some guilt. It was a little embarrassing to show up at the patient's home with the police. What does that say to patients and their families? I wished I didn't have to take the police along, but I knew I couldn't go without them. I continued to feel badly about this as time went by.

I had been talking to my parents about the job and they had serious concerns. They believed that my dad should tag along just to see what was going on and to ensure that I was safe. So I had driven to my parents' home and picked up Dad that day. He had on jeans and a dark blue jacket. I could see a bulge in his jacket above the waist on the right side. I knew what was there.

My father is not a big man but he is in fair shape for his age and he is streetwise. We set out for the East St. Louis police station, which looked easy to get to from the highway and on a map, but as we got into the area was hard to find. Thankfully the policewoman was familiar with the area and eventually we arrived.

I walked up the back steps to the back door and announced that I was Tia, a hospice nurse, and I went inside. The policewoman and my father did not follow me. They walked to the group in the back yard.

Once inside the very small kitchen, I visited with a daughter of the deceased man. After a minute or so, I saw my father poke his head in the door to inspect what was transpiring. He gave me a short wave and disappeared. The kitchen was full of people. Some had soda, others had beer. Food in casserole dishes lined the counters. The room smelled like a good hometown restaurant, but with smoking allowed.

The people in the kitchen briefly grew quiet when I walked in, but then quickly went back to their visiting.

The man who had passed away had been old, and he had been sick for a long time. Feelings and reactions tend to be different when an older person fades away gradually, as compared to the sudden death of someone younger. This explained the mood of the people who were there. This was an expected death. I relaxed a little, thinking that the mood would be fairly reasonable. After getting an update from the daughter, I went into the small bedroom where the patient had passed away.

The patient's room was quite small. A queen bed was pushed against the wall, leaving just enough space to walk in and out of the room. There was no space for other furniture. The only light in the room came from an old electric space heater on a folding TV tray next to the bed.

An old man leaned over the bed, staring at the deceased patient. He didn't move when I entered the room or even acknowledge me. His demeanor seemed quite different than all the other folks in the home. I took a second to adjust and then put my hand on his shoulder and said, "I am so sorry for your loss." I *was* sorry. I am always sorry.

He continued staring at the dead patient and then finally looked at me and said, "He is my brother." He then turned right back to his brother. I remained silent, giving him some time. I looked at the patient. The two looked close in age, and it was clear they were brothers. They had the same features, but of course, the deceased patient's face was sunken from the disease.

After a short time, the brother moved away from the bed and looked me right in the eyes. "He is my twin brother," he said.

"That must make this really hard for you," I replied.

He just nodded. As he straightened up his body, I explained that I was Tia from hospice and that I was there to help his family deal with the situation. He then gave his brother another last look and went into the kitchen. I thought how hard it would be to lose a twin.

I have known some twins. Quite often, twins are more than best friends in life. They tend to develop a very special relationship and a closeness greater than that between siblings. It occurred to me that he might be dealing with the concern that, if his brother had died, he might also die soon. That's a lot to deal with.

I finished the tasks that we hospice nurses normally perform upon a patient's passing and went into the kitchen. The mood was the same as when I had arrived. There was no sign of the brother, but that didn't surprise me. He most likely wanted to be alone.

I talked to the patient's sister at length, ensuring that all arrangements were made and also to let her know that we have grievance counselors available in case the brother or anyone else needed them. She was sharp and on top of things. She thanked me for all my help and we hugged.

Several people in the kitchen said goodbye to me as I headed out the door. As I opened the screen door, I stepped on the hind leg of one of the dogs. The screech let everyone in the back yard know I was coming out. I am a somewhat clumsy person. While walking over to my father, who was visiting as if he lived in the neighborhood, I heard a gunshot.

My brother and dad are hunters, so I know what a gunshot sounds like. I had shot rifles and guns when I was younger. This shot was close. Then I heard another shot. I ducked both times. I looked around at the crowd. They grew quiet for a moment and then started their conversations right up again. *Wow!* I thought. It didn't seem to bother them that bullets were flying just down the street.

I looked for the policewoman, thinking she would be running to her car and catching those bad guys with the guns. Instead, she was leaning on someone else's vehicle, visiting with a couple of guys. I wondered if I was maybe the only one who'd thought there were gunshots. *Where was my father?* I looked around and finally saw him heading my way.

"Did you hear those gunshots?" I asked him, thinking that maybe I was crazy.

"Yes," he said. "The folks in the crowd also heard them, and they remarked on how close they sounded." So it wasn't just me after all.

"If you're finished, we should leave," he said.

We assumed the police officer would follow or lead us out, so we walked over to her. However, she explained that her shift had ended about twenty minutes earlier, and since she lived just a few blocks over, she would be heading home.

Dad had made a few new friends, so he went to them to get the safest directions out of the area. Almost everyone said goodbye to us and several told us to be safe. We headed out, hoping the directions were solid.

They say that men aren't good about directions, but that day my dad had no problem. We shot out of the area, rolling through every stop sign. In a very short time, we were on the highway.

Safe in the car, I was able to reflect upon the sadness of the situation. As we drove to my parents' house, Dad and I discussed the twin brother and reflected on how hard it would be to lose one's lifelong twin. We talked about how we both get to go home to a safe place to live and we compared this to the grim conditions we'd just experienced. We agreed that I would only be allowed to go into unsafe areas accompanied by security or police—or I would have to quit my job. I continued to visit this region for some time, but eventually moved over to the other side of the river to Missouri.

At this writing, I have been conducting my hospice duties in these areas for about three years and have turned down many chances to move to other—safer—areas. For whatever reasons, I love the challenge of making sure my patients get equal or better care than all of our other patients citywide. I also like the openness and candidness of my patients. I feel they appreciate me as I help them get through what might be the most difficult time in their lives.

CHAPTER 2
Little Red Riding Hood in the Hood

One day, I rolled up in my little red Audi to a patient's home. John, my security, followed behind me in his all-black, all-tinted Tahoe. I went inside and tended to all of the patient's needs. She was an especially nice person and was always so concerned about my safety. It touched my heart that, as my patients were dying, so often they worried about me. After I told her where I had been on visits earlier that day, this patient commented that I go places even she and her family are too afraid to go. We said our goodbyes and her brother walked me out the door. He was about fifty, somewhat short, and a real gentleman.

"Be safe," he advised as he stood on the porch. "There's some white trash living across the street."

He noticed John in the black Tahoe. "Who's that?"

"That's my security," I assured him.

"Well, people around here must think you are FBI or DEA, because they know you wouldn't roll up here in your bright red car by yourself," he laughed. "I'm going to call you 'Little Red Riding Hood in the Hood.'"

I laughed at this, then we laughed together.

My car is bright red, my watch is red, my phone cover is red, and my shoes are red. I have been a huge Washington Redskins fan since I was a child and their colors are red and yellow.

Just as I was walking off the porch, we both heard a lady yelling. She was holding a small bottle that I immediately recognized. She was holding the container aloft and screaming at another lady a couple of houses down, a woman who was about to get on the city bus that was stopped at the corner.

"You forgot your bottle!" she yelled.

The bottle she held was one that you pee in for a urine sample. I have seen thousands of them. She yelled one more time as all the neighbors were now looking.

The other woman stepped off the bus and screamed back, "I don't need it 'till Thursday!"

My friend on the porch just shook his head. He told me that the friendly neighbor had been supplying her with clean urine samples for drug tests. We laughed because they didn't seem to care that the whole neighborhood knew what they were doing.

My friend shook his head and said, "Tia, welcome to the hood. All the bad things in the hood begin with 'h'—hookers, hustlers, hash, heroin and hoodlums."

Victor Hugo said, "If a soul is left in the darkness, sins will be committed. The guilty one is not he who commits the sin, but the one who causes the darkness." There is much darkness in these neighborhoods. There are also many great people. There is love, laughter and hope. There is an abundance of well-educated individuals and solid families.

There is greatness here. Since the obstacles are greater, those who make good must have had to overcome more than anyone would outside these areas. On a relative basis then, they are heroes.

These areas exist because our forefathers created the darkness by treating a group of fellow human beings as if they were inferior—as if they were not as human.

Things are still broken.

While African Americans live everywhere in our country and the world, these broken neighborhoods exist in most major cities. Other ethnic groups have their own version of these neighborhoods. Hispanics, Asians, whites, etc., usually have areas in major cities that feature similar social and economic conditions. In these areas, the same issues exist—issues that are not strictly related to race; they are related to poverty, lack of education, lack of employment, and discrimination.

When compared to middle-class white areas, the same proportions of people in poverty-stricken, disadvantaged neighborhoods have the same hopes, dreams and aspirations for their lives. The difference seems to be found in lack of real opportunity, greater obstacles, and an ongoing but necessary focus on basic survival.

My African-American clients and their families want, as we all do, to have a normal family, good schools, a safe neighborhood, and a good career where they can make enough money to live comfortably. As it turns out, as many of them are able to do this as compared to whites in other neighborhoods—where there are the same opportunities or obstacles.

I've learned in my work in disadvantaged neighborhoods that poor African-American communities and poor white communities have many of the same issues. In both, there are many wonderful people who go about their daily activities, just doing the best they can. And in both poor black and poor white communities, there is the "dark side." My experience of the dark side of some of the African-American neighborhoods applies equally to any poor white area. The only differences are cultural. The cultures are different, but neither is better nor worse.

CHAPTER 3

John Riggins, Soccer and Gommie

I was born in the Midwest to a middle-class family, and I had a fantastic childhood! I was surrounded by my parents, my brother, twelve aunts and uncles, and tons of cousins as well as good friends. Never a problem in school, I maintained above-average grades but had to work for them.

Early on, I took to sports. I played softball, volleyball, basketball and soccer. I became a solid swimmer and ice skater. I was competitive and loved the fun of being on a team. I also became a fan of football after watching games with the family on Sundays. Because of John Riggins, I became a lifelong Washington Redskins fan. I was not just "a little bit" into sports. Sports consumed me. Growing up in the town where I lived, there was one stand-out sport. The local high school boys' soccer team had gone to State and won several times while I was growing up. When I was eight years old, after two years of soccer, I landed on a team with a Hall of Fame soccer coach, Ruben Mendoza. He was a fantastic coach. He absolutely knew what he was doing, and I could tell he loved the game. Soccer became serious for me at that point.

Soccer became my game. I went on to play almost eleven months out of the year all the way up through high school and some college. My mom, brother and dad all played as well. We were a soccer family. I played on a traveling soccer team, played both indoor and outdoor, attended soccer camps in the summer and made the varsity team as a freshman, playing a full four years. While our team never won a state championship, we were the first girls' team to go to the state tournament from our high school. We won several regional and sectional titles along the way.

After high school, I was a little burned out on soccer. About a year later, a good friend told me to try out for the junior college team she was on. I got the job and scored three goals in the first game, immediately becoming a starter. Our team went on to play in the national tournament where we came in third in the nation.

I still play the game when I get a chance. I played pick-up games while working in Las Vegas and still play some indoor soccer with two of my best friends, Jennifer and LeAnn. We grew up together and—thank god—we still hang out and have great times. I believe the luckiest people are those who are able to keep the friends they had growing up, especially the special ones. (Also, they are both kick-ass soccer players!)

As a young child, I became especially close to my great grandmother. We called her Gommie. Gommie was old. She must have been seventy-five or so at the time. Back then and even today, I see a lot of people who are afraid of older folks, but I had no fear. For some reason I gravitated to the elderly. This may have been when I found my calling. While others around me felt a little uneasy around not just Gommie but all older people, I was comfortable. I talked to her with no reservation. I loved seeing her, and of course, Gommie seemed thrilled every time I was around. I felt I just had a gift with communicating with older people.

While in high school, I got a job at a nursing home and also earned my CNA (Certified Nursing Assistant) license. I soon took a job doing in-home care for a wonderful elderly lady. I did this until she passed away a couple of years later. While still in college, I took a CNA position at one of the top hospitals in the country.

I was studying to be a nurse. I was able to get into the nursing college that was supported by a major hospital. I graduated and took a nursing position at the hospital. After a couple of years, I decided to be a traveling nurse and worked in St. Louis, Fayetteville, Phoenix, Los Angeles, San Francisco, Burbank and Las Vegas. I mainly worked as a hospital nurse, but also had a position in a clinic and was a nurse manager in a nursing home.

In some of the jobs, I stayed a couple of years; in others, only months. It was great experience and as a result, now I have friends all over the country.

After having been in Las Vegas a couple of years, I decided it was time to go home and make a change. I packed up my stuff and the kitties, got in Lola (my car) and headed home. I was always intrigued by hospice, so I looked for and soon found a position.

Hospice nursing was a change alright. It was wildly different!

That was a few years ago.

CHAPTER 4

Neighborhood Watch-Out

It was just another day at work, and I was driving down the street headed to a patient's home. This particular morning was cold, but the Starbucks coffee was doing its job, and I was feeling good. John, of course, was following right behind me in his black Tahoe to make sure all would be safe. All of the sudden, a Mercedes blocked me off and on the other side, a BMW. Thinking back, it must have looked like an expensive used-car lot right in the middle of the neighborhood. Lola is an Audi, John has his big black Tahoe, and then there were the Mercedes and the very fine BMW.

That's not, however, what I was thinking at the time. I was wondering what the hell was going on. There were women in both of these cars. I stopped because I had to, and John sprang into action. As he was beginning to make his move, the lady in the Mercedes started to yell at me.

"What the hell are you doing in our neighborhood?" she screamed. "You don't belong! All you white people do is come in here and buy drugs and look for prostitutes."

"Get the hell out of here!" the lady in the BMW called out.

John was closely monitoring the situation. He had taught me never to leave the car. The car is your safety and it is also a 2,000-pound weapon. At first, the ladies didn't realize that John was with me. His Tahoe is not a totally foreign car for the area.

I was finally able to get a couple of words out and yelled back at the ladies through my partially cracked-open window. "I'm a hospice nurse and I'm headed to see a patient just down the street!"

By this time, they must have figured out that John was with me. They lowered their voices but continued to explain that the whites come into their neighborhood and drag it down by picking up prostitutes and buying drugs

John told me to head off to the patient's house. Since my window was down, I could hear both of them in harmony telling John about all the problems that the whites were causing in their area. John remained cool. In the mirror I could see him just nod politely—and then get the hell out of there. We both drove a little faster than usual to the patient's home. Once there, we just looked at each other for a few seconds. This whole episode had been a little scary and weird, and there were confusing feelings around it. These women were trying to improve a pretty desperate situation. They were working to make their communities safer and stronger. How can someone not admire that, even though they had yelled at John and me? Then, as we always do, we reviewed all the safety lessons that should have been learned and just shook our heads. I finally went in to take care of business with the patient.

I reflected that, though scary, this was a fantastic learning experience for all of us. These women were heroes. You have to really care to believe that you can make things better and make people more safe in your community. I bet those women have accomplished a lot of good. I didn't care that they were dead wrong about me and John and our intentions. What was cool was that they cared and knew what they had to do to be effective in getting the white drug buyers and white guys looking for prostitutes out of their neighborhoods. What makes the job even tougher for these ladies is that they are also the enemy of all the drug pushers and pimps and prostitutes in their area. This makes their job even more dangerous.

They had profiled me and I was okay with that. It is a necessary part of their mission. They profile to survive.

CHAPTER 5

The Man Who Takes Lollipops from the Bank

One day during my first year on the job, I was cruising through a really tough neighborhood heading to one of my patients who lived in an apartment building. I took John-the-security-guy with me that day because of previous experiences I'd had in this neighborhood.

Visiting homes in dangerous neighborhoods is tough going and visiting apartments in these areas can be even more dangerous. It is much harder to get in and out of apartment buildings, and a lot of people are walking and running around in the hallways. At this point, I didn't know John very well. He was always nice, polite, and kind of serious, as he should be. I rolled up to the apartment and he parked just behind me.

I entered the apartment and had pretty much completed my duties and was visiting with the patient's daughter. As we talked, she kept looking out the window. Finally, she stared at me.

"Where's your car?" she asked.

"It's the red Audi parked in front of the building," I said. "Why?"

"I'm going to call the police right away because the whole time you've been there, there's some guy parked right behind you!" she said, clearly worried. "I think he might be stalking you."

"Oh, he's with me! He's my security!" I said, laughing, and she looked surprised but then started to laugh, too.

"Well, then I want to meet him!" she said, walking out with me to his car.

John stepped out as the daughter introduced herself. "And who, may I ask, are you?" she smiled.

"I'm her boyfriend, and I follow her to make sure she doesn't cheat on me," he said. He delivered these lines perfectly and with a straight face.

"Well, there should not be a problem here, because I can see you are packing," she replied. And then she and I laughed. She looked at me again, smiling, and we both went into the apartment.

This was the first time I had ever seen John loosen up.

My initial meeting with John occurred when I was in orientation with another nurse. I was riding along with that nurse on a visit and John followed us. The nurse had chosen to take John on this particular visit because the patient's boyfriend had gotten in her face on the previous visit. We arrived at the house and headed inside while John got out of his vehicle.

I was impressed with John. He was tall, had a black suit coat on, and wore dark sunglasses. He looked like he meant business. My co-worker introduced him to me and he noted that he would accompany us inside the home. The nurse offered an update on what had transpired on the previous visit.

The patient's boyfriend answered the door. He looked us over suspiciously and turned to John.

"What you doing here?" he asked warily.

"John is here because you threatened me on my last visit," said my colleague, looking the boyfriend square in the eye. "And I am here to take care of your girlfriend without being in any danger."

He hesitated, but then let us in. I was a little surprised that the nurse had been so direct, but she did manage to clear up a great deal with just a few words. Even today, I am always disappointed when family members and others just can't find a way to be cooperative when someone in the home is dying.

"I'll just wait in the living room to give the patient some privacy," John told us. He was calm, but his presence was powerful. At the time, I didn't know whether he practiced this or if perhaps he was just a very serious person. It didn't matter, because it worked.

The boyfriend, too, remained calm and I could see that he and my co-worker were developing a new relationship. It was one that would work for all.

After we left the house, the nurse turned to John. "Do you think I did the right thing, bringing you on this call?"

"It doesn't matter what I think," John told her. "What matters is how you feel and what you thought."

That's pretty cool! I thought. And I realized that he was right.

This nurse had not used security in three years. I see this from time to time at work. Nurses are sometimes embarrassed to use security. They feel it might be awkward with the family, and they know there is an expense involved. My view is that not only is it safer to have security, it is a good investment. One dead, wounded or raped nurse, and the accompanying issues and expense would be unthinkable. In addition, I think a nurse will do a better job if he or she is not afraid while taking care of the patient and the family.

These neighborhoods can be dangerous at times and our company has always been one hundred percent supportive with the use of security.

Not too long after our visit with the other nurse, I felt I was getting to know John a little better and he seemed to be putting up with me. I was headed to a patient's home and John was directly behind me. We got there, and as I was getting out of the car, he stepped out, attired in a tuxedo. He looked like the President of the United States—except he is white. He looked amazing! I could tell he knew it, too, otherwise why would he get out of the vehicle?

The people in the neighborhood stared and pointed at him. They poked at each other and were clearly. wondering what the hell was going on. Who is he? Who is that white girl? What is going on? Soon several people came out of their houses and got on their cell phones. I went up to the porch and the patient's daughter came out and smiled as she passed right by me and headed for John.

"Do you always wear a tux to work?" she asked him.

He straightened up, military style, and said, "When you are guarding a princess, you have to look special." He maintained that serious look as she shook her head and walked back to me on the porch. We laughed together as we went into the home.

John had a tux on because he was headed off to provide security at an upscale event. I usually am able to schedule calls with him with some advance notice, but on occasion it's last minute. Over time I realized that John does some very important work. We are very fortunate to have him available.

He seems to know almost all of the police officers in several districts. Many of them do secondary work for him through his company. He also does security work for the St. Louis St. Patrick's Day Parade, the Dogtown St. Patrick's Day

Parade, the Mayor's Mardi Gras Ball, and he has picked up dignitaries at the airport coming in from Ireland. Later I found out that he worked security for the Atlanta and Salt Lake City Olympics.

Several years ago, he did security work for the visit of the President of the United States, Barack Obama. This was before Mr. Obama had become president.

I can't help but appreciate how fortunate it is that John provides security for me and my fellow nurses. We have the best. The fact is, though, that we need the best, considering the potential issues we face. They can be life and death and we need someone with John's vast experience and skills.

Over time, as we grew to know one another, we worked together to keep our senses of humor while at the same time staying sharp and vigilant. We also always try to make the lives of the people we see a little better beyond what is necessary.

John always reminds me that we are just visitors in our patients' neighborhoods and in their homes. We may never be accepted, but we should always try. I can remember one very nice summer day. I think the weather put us in a good mood that day. It wasn't hot and it wasn't cold. I was on my way to a visit with John following in his car. We pulled up to the home and exited our vehicles. There were a bunch of young kids, mostly the family's grandchildren, playing football in the front yard. John walked right over to them. They stopped playing their game and just started talking to John. They had no reservations, nor did he. While I didn't hear what was being said, I could see all the smiles on their faces.

They greeted him as if he was their long-lost uncle. The conversation was lively. After a short time, John was also smiling and kidding around with the children. Maybe they had issued a challenge to him. The oldest kid had the ball and passed it over to John, who made a perfect catch that was immediately converted to a passing pose. I watched them all get on their respective sides and position themselves for a play. The game was on—not a well-organized game, of course, just a lot of passing the ball back and forth.

These children were little and African American, and John is big and white. Color didn't matter on that day. I got to the porch where my patient was waiting for me. We looked at the game going on and just smiled. As I thought about the day later, I realized that we had been to the home several times. Maybe John had gotten to know the family and their situation fairly well. He obviously felt comfortable and natural hanging out with the kids. Maybe he just loves football like me.

John was always ready to step forward and help people. Not only did he make an effort to connect with the kids when the opportunity occurred, there were other times when I saw him help people dig out cars buried in the snow.

As a result of the tuxedo incident, John sometimes calls me "Princess." I think maybe it's not really a compliment as much as it is to let me know that I think I'm special, not that he thinks I'm special. In any case I like it. He also calls me "White Chick."

One summer day, I stood by John's vehicle and talked to him through the window as he sat in the driver's seat. Suddenly a beat-up old truck sped down the middle of the street and slammed on its brakes only about a foot away from John's vehicle. There was smoke coming up from the tires, and I could smell burning rubber.

There were two young African-American men inside. The driver stuck his head out of the window and yelled, "Hey, White Chick!" As John opened the door, he told me to get down on the ground. He shot up from his seat and stood very tall, staring at the guys in the truck.

"Oh shit!" was heard as the truck tried to speed away. We laughed a little because the way they took off after seeing John was kind of funny.

That is why he sometimes calls me "White Chick."

John is a great ambassador for what is good in people. I have seen neighborhood residents walk up to him while he stands by his car or sits inside it. The people he meets tell their friends, and we hope it gets around that we are there to help the families—not to interfere with their lives. We are *their* guests.

John is always professional and serious when doing our business. He is a very relaxed and confident person, and he is very good at what he does. He is always teaching. I think he knows that I am somewhat "street-wise" but that I need to bring things to another level. I can remember times when I was afraid, but he remained calm and went about his work. One day as I was walking a short distance down the street to the home of my patient, a car full of young people barreled down the street. They saw me and slammed on their brakes only a few feet from me. As they screeched the brakes, the car slid to the curb right in front of me.

I stood frozen. I had no idea of what was about to happen. I really thought it likely that they were going to shoot me. They were so close I could see every detail on their faces and even read their tattoos. I could have stretched out my arm and touched them. At times like these, most of us forget everything we know we should do.

Before I could collect myself, John had flown out of his vehicle and made his presence known. He was amazingly fast and effective. The teenagers sped off, and I came back to reality. I appreciated once again that he is so good at what he does.

Another time I was in front of a patient's home and reaching over to get my bag out of the driver's seat. Four men seemed to appear from nowhere and were getting close to my car. When they got within a few yards, one of them said, "Hey, baby, you got any drugs in that bag?" I wasn't afraid—I knew that John would be on it. He was already out of his vehicle. As quickly as they had approached me, they moved on.

When dealing with "a situation," John never yells or says anything obscene, he just gets out in front to end the potential for bad stuff to happen. He applies the right amount of action—but only what is needed—for a positive resolution.

John is physically fit. He's not particularly young and he's not old; he is in the middle. I know his age and think that he looks and acts about ten years younger.

John eats junk! Here's a diet for you: McDonald's, Wendy's, Burger King, burgers, french fries, Baby Ruth candy bars, Toll House chocolate chip cookies—and all washed down with an ice-cold Pepsi. That's the meal of this champion. Of course a man can't survive on just junk—or can he? I have never seen him drink water, but at times he has replaced the Pepsi with some Arnold Palmer tea (non-alcoholic). So in a few words, his diet is "No Vegetables and No Water," with everything else hopefully fried. He may be a health freak at home, but this is what I have observed when he is in between our calls.

On another day, we were waiting for me to determine the location of a particular patient. That may seem strange, but some of our hospice patients are mobile. Sometimes they go places or at other times, they move from one relative to another. My patients can't hide from me. I always get family and friends' phone numbers when I have a roaming patient. In this case, the patient was at a friend's house instead of being at home for our visit. I was trying to track her down. So I was standing by John's vehicle waiting for a return call. John and I were pretty serious that day because there had been a lot of shooting the night before just a couple of streets over.

While waiting, we reviewed what I had heard, and as always, John had the inside scoop. I love listening to his information. He sometimes talks like those movie-star police and FBI people, with all the technical jargon.

While I do my patient calls, John usually listens to a variety of music or reads magazines. He likes to stay on top of the gun world, most likely because he is a trainer, and I know he has a boat that he enjoys at the lake on the few weekends he is off duty. On this day I could see the boating magazines and gun magazines on his passenger seat, but he wasn't flipping through them as he usually does. There was no magazine reading on this day. His head moved from side to side and he was sizing up all the surroundings. We discussed the shootings from the previous night and I could hear the radio playing smooth jazz softly in the background. He plays that for his more serious, somber moods. In contrast, I have heard a lot of Jimmy Buffett in the summer, and at other times, I hear the pop stations.

So as the magazines lay dormant, the slow music played and John totally focused on the surroundings, we talked about the seriousness of potential retaliation shootings. His demeanor had a sobering effect, and I became serious as well.

Suddenly he looked down the street, concerned. "Did you notice the newly installed barriers a few houses down?" he said, pointing. "Why would they put them there?"

I told him that I did not know, and he described in detail how the barriers will help the police do their job.

This was as gravely serious as I'd ever seen John. He then pointed to a big fence that enclosed the cemetery across the street from us and looked at me with his light blue eyes and said, "Tia, do you know why they put up those fences around that cemetery?" I said, "No." John said, "Because…people are dying to get in there."

He got me.

John has taught me to be "present" at all times. He says to be relaxed but intimately aware of all my surroundings. It is weird, but I have become somewhat of a student of "Living in the Moment," so adding his recommendations actually fits nicely with my own approach to life. I can best describe this philosophy as living in the moment but at the same time being totally aware of my surroundings.

John once spoke to our nursing staff at a meeting, offering a "safety lecture." The key points I remember were to always keep our cell phones charged, never to leave anything of value visible in our cars, never to park in a patient's driveway, always to park on the street where you can take off quickly, and to make sure your panic button works on your key chain so your car horn going off it can be a signal for him to run in the house in emergencies.

He also taught us what to do and what to say so that we can extract ourselves from the house if we feel unsafe. He taught us to always have an escape plan while in a home that is potentially dangerous, even if it means jumping through the window.

While most of our patients are just regular people, they will be the first to tell you of the potential dangers in some of their neighborhoods. These families have their own plans for safety.

John is one of those people who seems to have done everything or he knows a lot or a little about everything. This characteristic has helped him converse with my patients and their families. At times, he has had to come in the homes for my safety, and we agree on these occasions that we will just tell them that he is a supervisor or he is just checking on how I am doing my job.

John is able to transform into any position or assignment he is given and do it well. Although we wish security would not have to be present, this quality makes my patients and their families comfortable.

John never brags, and he is a great listener. One day when he was in the living room of one of my patients, I could tell that he was a little down when we left. I thought he would be happy, because he was playing with a couple of kids in the living room while he waited for me.

As we were leaving I asked him, "What is the matter?" He said that he just thought it was sad that those kids didn't have a better environment to grow up in. He went on to say that he had worked for the state for three years investigating child abuse cases. He eventually moved on to other work because of the sadness and lack of hope for the kids' situations. He'd been particularly frustrated with the families and parents of the children.

John cared about children and surprisingly, he could be somewhat childlike himself. One day as I got out of my car in front of a patient's home, I looked around at the tough neighborhood and felt grateful to have security. I glanced back at John as he exited his vehicle. He stood tall and looked serious—ready to intimidate any and all who might threaten me—except for one thing. There was a green lollipop sticking out of his mouth.

I walked up to him and said, "Where did you get that?"

"I took it from the bank. I always do," John said.

I just shook my head and went in to see my patient.

CHAPTER 6

Curb-Service Hospice

*M*ost healthcare providers do their work at a permanent setting such as a hospital, clinic or doctor's office. This is not the case with hospice nurses, who usually visit a variety of homes and apartments that change as their patient mix changes. Hospice nurses are unusually flexible in this regard, but occasionally, even the expected care site can change at the last minute, and I have learned to be ready for almost anything.

One day I received information from the office that I had a patient who needed attention. They advised me that it was vital to take security because there were reports of drug transactions in the immediate area. I was instructed not to provide any drugs to the patient at the time of my visit. I called John and we headed out. I was in a brand-new Audi A6—a loaner car from the dealership while my car, "Lola," received a tune-up. It was a beautiful day. We were ending the worst winter in thirty-five years and this was the first seventy-degree-plus day. The sun was out and I had the Audi's sunroof open. It was a huge car with that great "new car" smell. The car's interior looked like an airplane cockpit, with every possible feature known to mankind. The dealership had not asked me where I would be driving the loaner, but I was sure they would want me to be safe wherever I went.

Yes, life was good. I had a brand new Audi, the best weather in six months, and John right behind me in the Tahoe. We were good to go.

The patient's daughter called and informed me that they would have to meet me at a different location. I got the new address, told John, and we headed out. As I pulled up to the new address, I saw the patient in the car. The daughter explained that the patient, this girl's mother, had been kicked out of the house that the daughter's father lives in. I thought that it takes a heartless person to throw out a dying person, but I set aside my judgments because I knew I had to get down to business to care for the patient.

I told the daughter that we could just go into the house to fix up her mother. The daughter explained that there was no house to go into. She further explained that they really didn't know anyone in the neighborhood and that there wasn't anywhere her mother would be welcome.

All the while I was assessing the patient. She was middle-aged and was suffering with a terrible disease. I could see that there was a dressing in need of replacement under her blouse. What to do? Take care of business.

I realized I did not have extra bandages and the other items required in the loaner car. They were in my car in the shop. I asked John if he had a first-aid kit. He was somewhat caught off guard because he hadn't yet been included in the plan. He went to get the kit and brought it to me while I conducted the assessment through the open car door. I stood up straight and asked John if he had some blankets. By now, John was in his emergency mode. He knew I was going to make something happen. Even though he wasn't sure what I would do, he trusted that it would get results.

I told John that we were going to remove the patient's blouse to change the bandages, but that the patient's privacy needed to be protected. As we both looked around, curious onlookers gathered.

John suggested we sit the patient on the back of his Tahoe so that we could hold up the blankets there. I agreed. So off to the Tahoe we went with the patient. We hung our make-shift curtains and removed the patient's blouse. I opened John's first-aid kit. All the supplies were present and sterile, but the kit was old, very old. "The eighties are calling and they want your first-aid kit back," I chided him.

Providing care in such an unconventional manner was not a problem for me. I was always ready for the unexpected. My concern was really for the patient. I removed her blouse and inspected the wound. Everything about this case was sad, but I knew that the patient was looking at my face to see what I was thinking. She would see no negative reaction from me. I told her that I would get her fixed up and further, that I would make sure that a social worker would contact her daughter immediately to get her into a shelter.

I took care of business. That's what we do. When it was over, John and I just kind of looked at one another. So many things happen in these situations that it takes a while to process them. For any and every patient, all that matters to me is that patients are cared for and that we put in place a plan to make them as comfortable as possible until the moment they die. White, black, brown, rich or poor, everyone gets treated with respect and gets equal care—period.

It was important to me to see this patient again soon, so I contacted the daughter for directions to her new location. I had been optimistic because I thought that at least my patient would die in a home. I corralled John for this visit and we set off to her new residence.

Unfortunately, her new place was not so good. The house was in a very rough part of town on a bad street. Even from outside, I could see that this was a really unclean house. I parked, got out and did a little practicing with the panic button on my keychain to make sure John would respond if I punched the button while I was in the house. Then I went up to the house and knocked on the door. The patient, looking horrible—even worse than our previous encounter when she looked terrible—answered the door. Her condition was appalling, and I knew I had a job to do.

I asked how she was doing, but I couldn't understand what she was trying to say. None of what the patient was articulating made any sense. Her speech was all garbled. I backed her into the house so I could put her somewhere comfortable and make an assessment. A baby cried in the living room, and I could hear female voices from one of the bedrooms.

Seeing the baby in this environment saddened and distracted me, but I knew I had to block it out and take care of business. I tried once again to talk to the patient. Her responses made no sense, so I asked her what medications she had taken. She told me she had taken street drugs. We always have a concern about the drugs we provide. We must make sure they are only used by our patients. This is not negotiable. There is a concern that in some cases the medications may be sold or traded for street drugs. There is also a concern that some patients may be taking both. We had seen cases of this in the hospitals I had worked in.

Just as I was beginning to change the dressing on the patient's chest, a large man came into the house. He looked right at me said, "What the fuck are you doing here?" I immediately got up and moved toward the door while calmly telling him that I was a hospice nurse there to take care of the patient.

As a result of being scared to death a few times in the past, I always had an exit plan ready for these occasions. I moved around him and toward the door. While walking out, I explained that I would be right back.

I was really frightened. I made it to the porch and motioned for John to come inside the house, explaining on the porch that this guy who had just walked in didn't seem at all happy I was there. We went inside and the big guy looked at John and said menacingly, "Who the fuck are you?"

"I am with Tia so she can take care of the patient," John told him.

John also managed to convey to the guy that this was his only purpose and that he wasn't interested in anything else. The guy just kept looking out the window. It was weird and surreal. He didn't seem to fear that John might turn him in or whatever. There was an understanding.

With John there, I popped my head in the bedroom just to gain a better lay of the land. There were two girls fully clothed on the bed and two children in the room. They were lying there but were not asleep. The kids were just sitting around but were not doing anything. This was very sad to me.

While John made friends with the small child in the other room, the man just kept looking out the window so I got to work tending to my patient. I asked for her pill bottle. There were two bottles which should have contained a week-and-a-half supply of medication. One bottle was empty and the other one seemed to have a foreign substance in it, so I asked the patient what had happened to the drugs, knowing that there was little chance of getting a coherent answer. I pretended that I understood what she was saying and explained that, based on the original doctor's orders, I could not supply any more medication.

The patient was totally out of it. I told her I was going to change her bandages. The patient said that she had put new bandages on herself. I opened the blouse and saw that the same bandages were on her chest that had come from the back of John's Tahoe a few days ago. I removed the bandages and saw that the wound site was horrible. This was not the worst that I had ever seen, but it was the second worst and the smell was putrid. What made this especially bad was the situation that this human being was in. If she were in a hospital, a nursing home or a real home, there would have been the means to improve the whole situation.

What do you do in these circumstances? Through the years as a hospice nurse, I have learned not to judge. You must be really patient and calm with the patient and the situation, and you must do everything possible to comfort them and to treat them with dignity. I explained that I would be talking to her daughter and the social worker to try to get her into a care facility as soon as possible. I looked her in the eye and asked her to please help herself as much as she could, and I reminded her that there were a lot of other folks who would help her do that.

I knew there was very little hope. Even though I had done everything I could, I knew that it was unlikely that this patient would die with dignity and without pain. Just as desperate as the situation was with the patient, there were also the children. I hoped that social services would be able to help their situation as well.

Music is a world within itself
With a language we all understand
With an equal opportunity
For all to sing, dance and clap their hands
But just because a record has a groove
Don't make it in the groove
But you can tell right away at letter A
When the people start to move
—*Stevie Wonder, Sir Duke*

CHAPTER 7

My Audition for a Job

While part of my job as a hospice nurse is to assess the patient, at times, they and their families are likewise assessing or "screening" me. Some initial nursing visits can be a job interview of sorts, and once I even "auditioned" for my job with a Stevie Wonder song.

That day I had been up two hours earlier than usual. I'd had a hard time sleeping the night before. During a meeting at work the day before, I'd found out that I was assigned to manage the case of a patient who was in his mid-twenties.

He had a terminal illness and had been sick for many years. When we went over his story, my co-workers all looked at me with compassion and sadness. I had never taken care of a patient that young during my hospice career.

I like old people but find it too sad to take care of sick children or babies. I knew that taking this assignment would be difficult. At this point in my career, I had only been doing hospice nursing for about two years, and I had never taken care of a person this young. I rose early that day with this patient on my mind, thinking about how young he was and trying to prepare myself for the journey.

We all think it is unfair when younger people die, so I figured my concern was normal. I made a cup of coffee and reviewed his records, got dressed and was on my way. I had called and spoken to his mother the day before to set up a time and she had suggested this early visit.

When I got to my location, I could see that this was a very nice, well-maintained home. The neighboring homes were also tidy and well kept. The streets were cleaned up and weeds had been pulled from the cracks in the sidewalks. I got out of my car and walked up through the well-groomed lawn.

I wasn't nervous; it was too early. A beautiful black woman answered the door. She had long wavy hair, fashionable slacks and a perfectly pressed blouse. She was so impeccably dressed that I couldn't help but look her up and down. By the time my eyes got to the perfectly matched red pumps she wore on her feet, I was fully awake. This was a classy outfit, and I looked down to compare it to my own scrubs and tennis shoes.

I guessed that this was the patient's sister. The woman extended her hand and said, "My name is Tina. I am Robert's mother. Come on in."

The inside of the home was beautiful. The décor reminded me of Italy. I had been there a couple of times. The home had what looked like Italian tile on the floor and several paintings and sculptures that appeared to be European. The tasteful furniture was perfect for the room. The colors were welcoming, with different walls painted various colors, but it all coordinated perfectly.

I followed Tina through the living room and we entered the family room, where a young man, my patient, was lying in one of those expensive "Posturepedic" type beds. Tina said, "This is my son, Robert." As I looked at him he cranked up a giant ear-to-ear smile. He lit up the room and that relaxed the hell out of me.

As I panned the room, I could tell that this mother got Robert everything that he wanted or needed, and this also made me smile. He had a complete entertainment center with a sixty-inch flat-screen TV and tons of video games that were organized like a library on the walls. I also saw a number of electronic gizmos that appeared to be recording equipment.

I introduced myself, and Tina asked me to have a seat. I sat down in a nice plush-velvet chair that matched the living room furniture. This chair was next to Robert's bed. Tina was very polite, but I could tell she wanted to get down to business. I saw a notebook and a pen on her lap. I asked her if she had any questions for me.

She said she did not because she understood what hospice was about. Then she said, "I want you to understand that Robert is my son, the light of my life, and I want the best for him." I assured her and Robert that our service was going to provide the best care for him and the family. Then she asked me about my nursing background.

This was a first for me and took me somewhat by surprise. I had never been asked this and I was delighted to give her the whole thing. I am proud of my career, and in a way I thought it would give her more confidence in me. Then I realized that she was actually interviewing me. While she fired away with questions, I noticed video cameras in the corner/ceilings of the room.

She completed the questions and seemed satisfied. Then she told me that she had hired a private-duty nurse to stay with her son for eight hours a day even though she was also at home during the day. She remained fairly serious, so I did, too.

Then she told me that she'd noticed me looking at the cameras. She explained that they are in the room so that when she is not there she can keep an eye on her son. She told me that, after several attempts, the private-duty nurse situation just hadn't worked out.

We had spent a great deal of time talking, so I thought this might be a good point to show her what we do. I asked her if it was okay if I assessed her son. She gave me the okay, so I went to work. I decided to focus on the patient and direct as much of the communication to him as I could. He was my focus. I did this naturally because he was the reason I had come there.

At first I was a little concerned that the interview might not have been over. She sat down the pad of paper and watched my every move. I did the head-to-toe check with all the vitals covered and then went into a fifteen-minute conversation with Robert about his medication. He loved the attention and could communicate pretty damned well for his condition.

I didn't know it at the time, but the mother really liked the way I shifted away from her to her son. He was totally capable and knowledgeable about his needs and issues. He was used to being poked and prodded. Just when I thought his smile couldn't get any bigger, he added a perfect laugh to it as he made a few jokes. As I was finishing up on the opposite side of the bed from his mother, he looked at me and said, "Tia, my mom is harmless, she is just overprotective."

I put my hand on his and said, "That's good, she should be." Hearing this, his mom smiled.

Robert and I then discussed our plan of care and the schedule of my visits. As I was wrapping things up, Robert said, "Do you like Stevie Wonder?"

I told him that I did.

He looked at me kind of puzzled and said, "What is your favorite song?"

Before he finished the question, I blurted out, "Higher Ground."

He brought out one of those great smiles and his mother even smiled. He reached over immediately, hitting all kinds of buttons on the console to his right. And then it happened—the music started. He began sliding up the volume controls and the room started to shake.

I couldn't believe what I saw next. Tina started moving to the music. What the hell was going on? As far as I was concerned, this signaled that the interview was over. Robert started singing and then Tina started singing, so I just jumped in, too. Robert watched my lips and could see I knew the words perfectly. When the song ended, we all congratulated one another on what great singers we were. They seemed surprised but delighted that I had joined in. I have a message for African-American people everywhere. White people listen to your music. We know your music well. This was not the first time that I had surprised my black patients or friends with the fact that I know the songs.

My dad once told me a story that I still remember. My mom had gained a few pounds after her medical treatments. My dad had retired to be at home with her and it was close to the time that he was ready to do so anyway. My mom decided to join a gym that included "Zumba" classes. Once they had the membership, my mom told him she was signing up for the "Zumba" and asked if he was willing to go. He said he would.

So there is my father in a room with thirty women—almost all of them white—dancing to the music for an hour every week. The instructor was African American and everyone got along beautifully with her. Several class members went to dinner with her, and they eventually had a birthday party for her.

As my dad told it:

"Michael Jackson died on the same day one of the classes was taking place. All of the members were there before the instructor came in a little late. She looked sad. I think some of the class members assumed that this may have been the result of the Michael Jackson's death. Nothing was said at first. One of her best friends in the class mentioned it to her and she acknowledged it.

"The room went quiet. After a little silence, one of the ladies suggested that it would be great if she wanted to put on some Michael Jackson music. Our instructor always carried a case of CDs. The instructor's face went from sadness to a tearful smile. I watched her look around the room at our all-white faces. She seemed amazed that we were so thoughtful. So she dug through the CDs and laid out a few of them on the floor next to the audio system. The music began and we all started our now-very-familiar routine moves that had been the same every week for the full hour.

"After the first song, she asked if it would be okay if she played another. We told her it was, and so for the full hour, we all listened to Michael Jackson's music. About halfway in, she put on one of those Michael Jackson songs that everybody not only knows the words to, but also the moves. The instructor was in the front of the class and had her back to us. We followed her moves as we looked into the mirror in front of her. These were the same moves we had done every week for a full hour.

"Suddenly, however, she broke out into Michael Jackson moves that fit the song. She just couldn't help herself. Since we were all glued to her moves for the entire hour every week anyway, we just followed her. Then we all started singing. We all knew the words and knew most of the moves. It was wild when all the white people did the graveyard zombie walk. She stopped in the middle of the song, went over and shut off the music, and stood right in front of us, staring.

"She started to cry and said, "You guys know this stuff?" One girl went up and hugged her. The instructor hopped over to the audio equipment and fired it up. For the next hour we had a Michael Jackson dance party."

My father was asked if he could "Moon Walk." The members knew the moves and the instructor danced and sang the whole hour. Heck, my mom is still a Motown fan, and just recently I was reminded that I'd bought a "Michael Jackson" jacket when I was a kid. It was red, of course.

The point is, when someone is dying, they and their families don't have time for pretense or pettiness and at this time they tend to speak honestly and "cut to the chase." In this way, death strips away the color of our skin. But it occurred to me that music and singing and dancing together also do the same thing. They allow us to be joyful and to celebrate with one another. Maybe this is the "Higher Ground" that Stevie Wonder sang about—any place that allows us to be genuine and loving human beings with one another. I saw this with Robert and Tina, and my dad saw it with his Zumba class.

After our spur-of-the-moment concert, it was time for me to leave Tina and Robert. We were all in a good mood. Tina walked me to the front door and told me that she thought I would be a good fit for them. I had passed my "audition."

Over the period of time that I took care of them, I learned important lessons from this family. Robert and his family were laser-focused on positive things. They lived life in the moment and they lived it to the fullest. With the help of his family, Robert was living a full life in half the time that most of us have been given. Most important, Robert had one of the best attitudes I have ever experienced, and it was uplifting simply to be with him.

I felt wonderful on the drive to my next visit because I had expected the worst and instead found a patient with a terrible condition who was getting the best care possible. After I finished that visit, I went to my trunk and rifled through my CDs. There it was: "Stevie Wonder." I actually had two of his CDs. I got in Lola and cranked up the music. While I sang "Higher Ground," it now had new meaning for me. All my songs have meaning to me and make me remember something or somebody. "Higher Ground" was Robert's song now and it will forever be him I think of whenever I hear it.

My job is the medical side, but many families let us in to some of the other sides of their lives, which helps them cope through the dying process. I visited Robert and his family over the next six months. I got to know them all, and each one of them was a fantastic individual. Robert was not only playing music when I would arrive, he was also creating his own, and he was really good at it. I later learned that he was fairly advanced as a musician/composer. He also loved video games. He seemed to find real joy in these things. The damned kid was happy all the time! He found something that I am still looking for. Maybe we are all looking for it: Higher Ground.

There were times when he had some pretty tough issues and he would tell his mom to call Tia. Fortunately, we were usually able to get him back on track quickly, but over time he started to fail. I shouldn't have, but I had become close to the family. Anyone would have. They let me in.

Tina had hired a caretaker once she saw him fading. I was under the impression that things were going fairly well with the caretaker. One day I showed up for my regular visit and Tina greeted me at the door. She was not her normal self. I asked her what was wrong.

"That person I hired was terrible," she said, clearly agitated. "She was always late and didn't do anything for my son."

"I'm so sorry to hear that it did not work out," I said, trying to comfort her.

She collected herself. "I fired her ass this morning," she told me. "Tia, you have to check yourself before you wreck yourself."

"Check yourself before you wreck yourself," Tina had said. I always liked that saying and have used it many times as my own mantra since I first heard it from her.

Tina sat on the couch in the living room and I sat across from her in the chair. She grew teary eyed. "Tia, I am not a weak woman," she said. "I have my own business. I have taken care of Robert. I got my master's degree as soon as I found out he had the illness. When all the young punks started selling drugs on the corners, the neighbors all got together and we put a stop to it. It was like the 'Harper Valley PTA' up here. I don't let things get me down because I have to be a role model for my son. Does this situation suck? Yes, it does, but I am not going to curl up in a ball and get myself down."

I moved over and sat next to her on the couch. "You are one of the strongest people I have ever known," I told her. "You have raised Robert with such love and compassion, it's unbelievable! Most people would have just felt sorry for themselves. You went in the other direction. You and your family live life to the fullest every day."

The word had gotten out about Robert's condition. We both went into the room which by now was filled with his friends. As I was walking in, one of Robert's cousins got up and introduced himself and said, "You're the Tia we have all been hearing about."

"Yes I am," I said.

He held an electric guitar in his hand and said, "Well, after seeing you, I am surprised you like Stevie Wonder. Robert said you sang along with him and his mom on 'Higher Ground' and knew all the lyrics, word for word."

I nodded and said, "Yes."

Robert was listening to our conversation and put his weak hands on the knobs, cranking up "Living Just Enough for the City." I was thinking that it had been a long time ago that we had sung "Higher Ground." Since then, I'd had many discussions with Robert about music and we must have listened to hundreds of songs. I even introduced him to some "white people" music.

Robert wasn't doing well and he really didn't have long to live, but that day he found the strength to control the music. The room was full of his family and friends and me. I immediately had a vision that we would all sing together as the music began to play. We would be like the group that sang the "I'd Like to Buy the World a Coke and Sing in Perfect Harmony" commercial, only we'd be singing Stevie Wonder.

The music started and I closed my eyes a little, getting ready to come in. Then the music stopped completely and—suddenly! I opened my eyes and everyone in the room was smiling, except for me. Robert's cousin looked right at me along with everyone else and said, "Okay Tia, what is the first line of the song?"

I took off my jacket and carefully put it across the top of the velvet chair. I slowly put my medical bag on the floor and then I belted out the first line with no music. Robert got one of those giant smiles on his face and brought up the music, and we sang the whole song together.

After we finished the song, Robert's cousin walked up to me. "Tia, you are no joke," he said.

"We are not sure where Tia comes from," Tina added.

When Robert died soon after, my whole office was concerned for me. His family held a huge celebration for his passing. I was consoled by the fact that this young man had been provided with more love than seemed humanly possible. In return, he left us his music and his great smile. As I think about it from time to time, the real story there was the love his mother had for her son. I see and hear from Tina from time to time. His love for music, his great smile, his determination to live a full life in half the time that most of us are dealt, and the special love and care his mother showed for him—these were the gifts that Robert and his family left me.

CHAPTER 8
Ted and Tia for President

On the day Ted died, I cried. Ted was one of my patients, and he had been a friend—a good friend.

There are people who come into your life and change you. Ted was one of those people for me. As I drove around that day, I visualized the last time I saw him. It was at his front door. He was letting me out of the house and holding the screen door and the regular door at the same time. He said, "Now don't you forget your old Uncle Teddy, Tia." I said, "Don't you worry about that."

What Ted changed in me was how I view all human beings. You may see people and you make a judgment about them based on how they look, where they live, how they dress, how they act and what others have told you about them. I learned that you can really be wrong when making assumptions about people. It takes time to really get to know someone.

Ted was one of my first patients. He actually lived outside the regular territory where I normally worked, but one day I got a call from my boss. She told me that they had a tough patient who had just fired one of our nurses and that she believed I was the perfect person to handle him.

My boss is a great lady. She had worked in the hospice field for a long time and had wonderful stories about taking care of patients and families in the far reaches of rural areas away from the city. I had only known her for a relatively short time, but we were absolutely on the same wavelength. She was tough like me, and we always cut through the crap when we had conversations. The greatest thing about her was that I always knew she had my back.

In my line of work, we all make mistakes and sometimes people just get attacked from all sides for no particularly good reason. This might have been the case with the nurse who had been fired. My boss was great because she judged everyone by their entire body of work—not just by one wrong incident or thing. If anyone reading this should happen to be a supervisor and you want to gain your workers' trust, just convince them that you will always have their back. The workers will respect you and move mountains for you.

My boss gave me all the background on the patient and the family. She said that the family was really great, especially the patient's wife.

I also had the opportunity to read the report from the nurse who was fired and could see that this patient was going to be tough. One issue was that he always insisted on choosing the specific time and day he would allow us to come by. Because we have so many patients and a busy schedule, we usually tell them when we are coming by. This is also important because I have to arrange for security to accompany me. Ted lived in an area we had labeled for security.

I called the home and he answered the phone, which surprised me a little because his condition was serious. I told him to pick a day and time that worked best for him. I agreed to the day and time he suggested and rearranged my schedule to make it work. The day of the first meeting, I went by Starbucks and got a fresh green tea, jumped in Lola and cranked up Kid Rock on the stereo.

I wasn't nervous, but I was gearing up for a challenge. I got there and was greeted at the door by Ted's wife, who introduced herself as Nora. She *was* nervous. I assumed this was because she did not know how Ted would respond to me. I introduced myself, and she informed me that her husband wasn't doing so well that day—he was in a great deal of pain.

Nora went on to say that Ted had called her at work to ask her to come home and do something—or anything—to help him. She said she was glad to see me and hoped that I could help.

I walked into the kitchen. To the right was a bathroom, and to the left I could see a makeshift bedroom that used to be the living room. The supposed mean guy was lying in a hospital bed in the center of this room. What the hell!

He was a little guy and was smiling at me. He had all his street clothes on except his shoes and didn't really even look like a patient. It occurred to me that maybe these were his fighting clothes. He was looking me over. I was wondering if maybe he thought I was fresh meat that he was getting ready to attack. If he was in pain, he gave no sign of it. Was he sucking me into a trap?

I couldn't get out of my mind the scene in that movie *The Exorcist* where the girl in the bed looks normal and then she spews green pea soup or whatever as her head spins 360 degrees.

Ted was a light-skinned African American. His mother was Cherokee Indian and his dad was an African American. He had beautiful grey-blue eyes. Actually, I also have a little Cherokee blood in me. My full first name is Tiatussa, and my parents named me after my mom's great, great aunt who had been a Cherokee princess.

Ted was short and had a normal build. He sat up and I introduced myself. I told him that my name was Tia and that I was going to be his nurse. He reached to his right, grabbed the top of a chair and moved it a little closer to his bed. Then he told me that the chair was for me and that I should take a seat.

I sat and he reached over to shake my hand. We began with a regular handshake, but Ted converted it to what I call a "brother's shake." My dad used to do this with me when I was a kid. You connect for the regular shake and then point your fingers straight up into the brother's shake and close. I took to it naturally with Ted because I had done it many times before. Then we did some side-to-side stuff and ended with a fist bump. Over time, we smoothed out all the elements of the handshake and this became our secret handshake every time I visited.

Ted didn't know me at all, but for some reason, he was determined to start things off right. I think that my ability to do the shake smoothly shocked him a little and also advanced us to a new level.

I asked him if he had any questions. He asked me if I was going to take care of his pain. I told him that together we would find a way to get it under control. I reviewed his medications with him and said that I would call the doctor and get an order to make the changes necessary to get the job done.

I told Ted that he was the captain of the ship and that I was just the GPS to help guide him on his voyage. I could tell he was interviewing me to determine if I was competent enough to take care of him. I felt he was giving me a chance to prove it.

He was so nice and so polite that I couldn't help but wonder what had happened to the previous nurse. We never blame nurses when they get fired. All of our nurses are wonderful, but sometimes, for whatever reason, the family or patient just feel they want someone else. We respect that, make the staffing change, and don't waste our time about the reason unless there is a legitimate complaint.

Just as I was feeling that things were going well with Ted, I heard a very loud screech from a child. A screaming three-year-old flew through the air, landing on the hospital bed and yelling, "Grandpa! Grandpa!" The child's mother ran into the room just behind him and shouted for the child to get off the bed. Then Ted sat up in the bed and grabbed a weapon (a cane from the other side of the bed). I was thinking I wish I had known *that* was there before.

Ted swung the cane through the air like Zorro in a perfect sweeping motion to try to scare the child but not get it anywhere near where he would make any contact. This was a choreographed move that I could tell had the practiced precision of having been done many times before. As he swung the cane, Ted yelled, "Get off my bed, boy!"

The child was yelling, the mom was yelling and Ted was yelling. None of this scared me. I could tell the boy loved his grandpa and was just messing with him. But during this encounter, I did see another side of Ted. He had sucked it up for me before, but it was obvious that his pain was bad.

The mother took the boy into the other room and Ted looked at me for a reaction. I remarked that he had a really cute grandson. Ted mumbled something and then collected himself. I told him that I was going to get on the phone to see if I could make adjustments to his medications, but I had a few more questions for him.

I then assessed Ted from head to toe. I asked him where the pain was, how often he experienced it, and whether he could describe the level of pain. He gave me very specific answers. I then asked him what he thought had worked in the past.

Ted was a different sort of patient—what normally works for patients in his situation was not working for him. His pain control would have to be customized just for him. I called the doctor and went over everything in detail, doing so in front of Ted so that he could hear what I was doing, and also so that he would be available if the doctor had any additional questions.

The doctor made the changes on the phone and said that he would call them in. I hung up and told Ted that the revisions would take place immediately and that the prescriptions were being called in at that moment. I told him that we believed the new medications would work and that I would follow up with him tomorrow.

I asked him for a time that would work best for him. We agreed on a time, did our new secret handshake, and then I left the room. I went over all the medication changes with Ted's wife. I could see they were hopeful for a better outcome. Nora and her daughter walked me out to the porch, remarking that they were grateful I had come. It seemed they thought I was a good fit for Ted's care. Nora noted that he had been very crabby and demanding, but that she knew it was because of the pain he had.

"Well, there's a new sheriff in town, and it's me. I will get that pain under control," I said, thinking that this might not have been a perfect thing to say. They both laughed and replied that that was exactly what Ted needed.

I called my medical director and also our nurse practitioner, and we did another review of the patient's chart and history of pain medications. While we typically make changes for patients, this one was challenging. We had already made several adjustments that had failed. The new approach was pretty dramatic—something new for all of us except for the physician. He had seen these situations before and knew how to adjust the medications to better address Ted's pain.

This was a learning experience for me. I had never seen a case where the body of a patient was not responding to the normal treatments and also not responding to secondary adjustments. I learned that there can be a vast difference in tolerance levels for reactions to medicines. Ted's case was unusual, and I hoped the medication adjustment would work. If not, I figured I would be fired from the case as my co-worker had been—or maybe I would be whacked with the cane!

I visited with Ted early the next day. I went into the house after saying my hellos. Nora was in the room and she gave me a report immediately. It seemed that maybe Ted was in charge of the house when he was in pain and all pissed off, but she was in charge of the rest of the time. I went over to Ted and he reached out and we did our now-not-so-secret handshake. Nora observed this and shook her head, indicating that "the shake" was just another one of those weird things her husband did.

Ted looked good. Nora offered a very detailed report about how they were seeing a little improvement for the first time. It was clear that they remained cautiously hopeful the new medication approach would work. Ted simply listened. He'd gone back into his submissive role as a "yes man" husband, I thought. Nora was well dressed and had most likely taken off work for my visit. While she talked, I noticed a complete outline of the plan we had discussed on a large dry-erase board hanging on the wall behind the bed. These were clearly some sharp, caring people who had their act together.

I told the family to call me if anything changed and that we would take it day by day. They walked me out after I had one more handshake with Ted. He didn't say much. He looked as if he was reading his body. It appeared as if he was trying to feel whether the medicine was working. He was preoccupied with it, I thought, and I left thinking that at least we had a chance

I didn't get any calls the next day from the family—no complaints and no calls firing me. I called the home and Ted answered the phone. He told me he was feeling good. I was very pleased to hear this and told him I could swing by at three for a quick visit. He said that was good. I noticed that for the first time, I was in control of when I would be visiting him.

I arrived at the house and rapped on the door. Ted himself answered the door. He looked great. My first thought was that maybe he was a little high from the meds. I walked in and followed him into what was now the bedroom. As I headed for the couch, I saw that cane thing guide me toward a desk and chair in the corner of the room. He said, "Sit there. That is your desk."

I looked more closely. They had set up a small, shiny wooden desk for me with a nice small chair. I could smell that it had recently been cleaned up with Pledge. It held a notepad, a coffee cup full of sharpened pencils, and a desk lamp. I pulled out the chair and sat down, and Ted headed to his bed to lie down.

He told me that, for the first time since the pain had started a long time ago, he truly felt better. I had completed all my calls for the day and had plenty of time to visit. We talked for a long time. He told me all about himself and his family. It was damned interesting! Ted had a wonderful family and he'd had a very interesting life.

I was thinking about how unlucky the fired nurse had been. It wasn't her fault, I thought. If the meds had been adjusted when she was making the calls, she would have been the one sitting at this wonderful office set up that was now mine.

Ted talked until I could tell he was getting a little tired. He reached over and turned on an old cassette player. I realized that this was in his routine. It's very common for people to soothe themselves with their favorite music as they are dying. I recognized the song and the group. Ted laid back and seemed to be in a good place.

"Ted, that's The Commodores, isn't it?" I asked.

"Yes it is, young lady," he said, sitting up. He turned up the song since he knew I liked it too. Then he started to sing as he lay back on the bed. He looked at me and I also sang the song quietly. He sat all the way up, reached over to the cassette player and rewound the song, and then cranked up the volume.

We looked at each other like Ike and Tina waiting for the music to let us know when to come in. Then it started. We hesitantly started to sing, but soon we were full blast filling the room and then the whole house with "Sail On." Neither of us missed a word, and we even used a few arm and hand gestures to liven things up.

It was a great moment. During that song, I hoped that Ted forgot for just a few moments about dying. And I forgot about all my problems. It was just fun.

The song ended and Ted just looked at me in wonderment. "Man, Tia you can do some singing."

"Ted, you have a kick-ass voice," I replied, and he thanked me.

Nora stuck her head in the door and said, "You two are crazy." She gave him the same look as when we had the handshake and then her head disappeared.

I told Ted that I had to go but was so happy that he was doing better. We did our handshake and then he reached over with his other hand and put it on top of our handshake—a super-sized secret handshake.

I went into the other room and Nora hugged me. She didn't say much, but she didn't have to. The doctors had figured this one out and we were good to go. As time passed, I became good friends with Nora. She is a fantastic person. I am as lucky to get to know her as I was to know Ted. She is the rock of the family.

It was dark outside when I finally left. I had stayed a much longer time than I thought I would, but it was worth it.

I made many other visits to Ted's house, and each time I got to know him and his family better and better. His family was wonderful. They took great care of him and most important, they followed our entire medical directions perfectly. I could tell that this was the way they did everything in their family.

My routine was to come over, perform my complete assessment, and then move into my corner office that Ted had prepared for me to enter all the information into my computer. Over time, the desk looked like a real work station. There were papers on it, along with some CDs and other stuff that Ted wanted me to look over. A couple of times there would be one fresh flower in a vase.

One particular day was just like any other day to visit Ted and his family. It was just really cold—that crisp kind of cold that no matter what you wear, you freeze as soon as you step out of the car. I sipped on my Starbucks one last time as I arrived at the home.

When I would go to see Ted, I never had any expectations other than hoping his pain was under control and hoping he was feeling good otherwise. He had the toughest pain management situation we had ever dealt with. We needed to constantly adjust the medicine to keep him comfortable, and he came to trust that we could always make it happen—and usually pretty fast.

Ted had his own philosophy of his condition. He would say that, "It is like a box of chocolates, you don't know what you will get each time you come over."

So on that cold day, I went to the door where Ted greeted me, but I could hardly hear what he was saying because the noise from inside the house was so loud. He had the radio blasting and he seemed very animated. It was on a talk radio station and some political figure was giving a speech.

"Just be quiet and listen to the words," Ted told me. "They are like poetry."

He pushed me with his cane over to my office in the corner and I sat down. He yelled to me over the sound of the radio, "It's like poetry!" Ted was right; this guy was going down a list of positive changes he wanted to make for the country.

Ted and I found another thing in life that we shared: our politics. We listened to every word that was said. We would nod in agreement every few seconds. This was no different than when we connected on the music. I thought that it was a good thing this was the case, because I didn't want to ruin our relationship or have that cane flying across the room at me.

When the speech was over, I went to work doing my assessment. While performing the work, we talked over one another for the entire time about how we would improve the country. I loved his ideas and he loved mine. I guess he knew me long enough that he just was able to make an assumption about my political views. We covered all the major issues facing the country and came up with multiple solutions.

At the end of our discussion, out came Ted's cane and into the air it went. "Let's run on the next presidential ticket. It will be 'Teddy and Tia,'" he said, flourishing the cane. I laughed at this, but at the same time thought what a blast it would be to do such a thing with Ted. We were sharing one of our great moments. I couldn't help but be awed that Ted was in the process of dying—and soon, of course—but he was talking about something that would happen years in the future. I am always thrilled when my patients talk about the future in a positive way.

This was my last call of the day so we had the time to lay out all of our presidential plans in detail. They were "kick ass."

Then I realized why I was enjoying the moment so much. It wasn't just because he was thinking about the future, but also that I had a period of time when I wasn't thinking about him dying.

As we were finishing, a head poked into the room. It was a daughter this time. "What are you two up to now?" she asked.

"Tia and I are running for president and vice president," Ted told her. "We are going to change the world." His other daughter entered the room and they both rolled their eyes at the same time.

Ted's daughters are really neat adult children. One of the them has a master's degree and the other is working on hers. They have also made many trips throughout the world. They had just returned from a trip to Israel and were planning their next trip to Paris. One of them had published a book and was working on another one.

Ted was very proud of them. I realized that he most likely had been very demanding as they grew up in the same way he was demanding of me.

As I completed my work, one of his daughters yelled from the other room, "There is some chick on Facebook that says Uncle Johnny is the father of her child."

"Let me see," said Ted. He grabbed her phone away as she came close.

He knew how to navigate on the cell phone. He hated modern technology but was smart enough to know how to use it. He pushed a bunch of buttons and then we all asked him what he was looking at. He told us to look at the picture on the phone. It was a black woman with several white people around her.

Then Ted said, "She is with some friends, it's a bunch of white people."

"So..." one of his daughters said.

"That's just to show us she has some white friends," Ted said.

This was interesting. I was thinking that I have heard white people say the same thing in reverse. They say that "so-and-so has a black friend" or "some of my best friends are black" just to show that they get along with African Americans. I was pleased that they all felt comfortable talking about all of this in front of me. I finished the visit with the secret handshake from Ted, hugs from Nora and both daughters, and then I headed home.

I had many more visits with Ted before his passing. Almost all of them were just as interesting and enjoyable. He was a special person. I still think of him and his family often.

I will never forget you, Ted.

CHAPTER 9

Yes, You in the Back Yard, Come Out and Answer Your Door!

Although John is usually my security escort, sometimes he has to take other calls or has other business to attend to. That was the case one day, so I called his office and talked to Tom, one of John's associates. We set up a time and place to meet. I met him in front of the patient's home. We arrived at the same time. I got out of my car and he did the same. He walked up to me and smiled.

Tom put out his hand and we shook. Tom was tall and thin. He dressed very much like John, wearing the black shoes, dress shirt and khaki pants. He was somewhat serious. I didn't know if that was his usual demeanor or the result of having just met me.

I told Tom that I would be in the house for about forty-five minutes and headed into the patient's home. I looked around cautiously while heading to the porch because an unusual amount of activity had been occurring over the past few days. There had been a lot of shootings. I walked up to the door and knocked. I wanted to get into the house quickly to avoid anything that might happen when I was outside and exposed. I knocked again—still no answer. After knocking several times, I looked over at Tom sitting in his vehicle.

He had his window down and I felt he was getting nervous. I stayed on the porch, committed to getting someone to answer the door. The family had told me on the phone that they would be there when I arrived.

By this time, there were cars speeding down the street and plenty of other activity, including several neighbors watching me. I was feeling a little nervous myself. I hadn't been on this street before. I gave it one more knock, but there was still no answer. Just as I was turning around to leave, I heard what sounded like a huge megaphone that could be heard from one end of the block to the other—and inside the houses, too, I'm sure. The message was, "Hey! You in the back yard! Answer your front door!"

I have never used this word before but this "startled" me. I had no idea where the booming voice was coming from. As I looked around, along with all of the other people in the neighborhood, I heard it again. The new message, even louder, was, "Yes, you in the back yard, answer your door!"

At this point all the rest of the neighbors were out of their houses. The door in front of me opened. There stood my patient's sister, laughing her ass off. I looked out at Tom and he gave me a thumbs up. Then I figured it out. Tom must have had some kind of CB or radio system with an outside speaker.

I admit it took me a minute to figure it out. The sister was still laughing. She said, "Miss Tia, you do whatever it takes to see your patient, don't you!" While I performed my duties, we laughed some more and then she asked me if John was okay. I told her that he was just on other business. We kept talking as I finished up, and then I walked out with the sister. She waved to Tom and he waved back.

This was interesting. We visiting nurses never try to draw attention to ourselves as we go about our business. I guess Tom was just getting the job done—and it worked. In any case, his antics made me laugh. In fact, it seemed that everyone had gotten quite a kick out of it.

I had another patient to see, so we headed off. This was a busy day on the streets. There were a higher-than-usual number of cars flying by. We got to my next visit and I headed to the porch, hoping the family would answer the door quickly enough so that Tom wouldn't be tempted to use his megaphone. Fortunately, they did respond quickly and I went inside. This was a very positive visit. I spent time with the patient's son, who was taking wonderful care of his father. He was a very impressive young man, and we got along very well.

I finished up, headed out the door, got outside, and glanced at Tom. He looked serious.

"Are you okay?" I asked.

"Yes, but we should get in our cars and move on," he said, so I climbed into Lola and we were off to our next patient visit.

When we arrived in front of the home, I got out and went back to Tom. "Are you sure you're alright?" I asked again.

"Yes, but it's been a long time since I've actually unholstered my gun and put it on my lap," he said. He went on to explain that once I had gone into the home, the activity on the streets had increased. There continued to be a lot of car traffic. Keep in mind that these streets were very narrow. As the cars pass, you are really close to them and they to you.

Tom could see that in front of his car, several people were coming out on the corner. As he looked in the mirror, he saw that behind him the same was true. We were in the middle of the block, which wasn't unusual. These kids, however, were out on bikes. One of them was riding his bike back and forth, getting closer and closer to his vehicle each time. Tom has been around and knew what this was. He told me what I already knew, which was that these kids were looking out for the drug dealers. Tom thought that the kid was attempting to keep getting closer to determine who he was and what he was doing there.

This was a tense situation because the kid on the bike was reporting back to the other older kids on the corner. Then the cars would drive by. Uncomfortable thoughts swirled through my head as I considered the situation. Maybe they were just unfamiliar with us. Maybe the next time we came, they would know who were and stay clear. Maybe it was just a good idea to be ready for anything.

A few days later I needed security, so I called and got Tom. I was getting to know him a little better, and I met him in front of my patient's home. It was a very nice sunny day—warm with just a little breeze. It was just right. It was Friday, but it wasn't just Friday. It was Friday and I didn't have to work on Saturday and Sunday. This would be my last call for the week.

On this beautiful day, I was just feeling really good. One more call and I would finally be off. I exited Lola—I had just washed her and she was looking sharp—and walked back to Tom's vehicle to say hello. As we walked up to one another, we heard the shots.

Pow, pow, pow, pow, pow...pow, pow, pow, pow, pow, pow...pow, pow, pow.

After the first shot, Tom had me in his car with the door closed as he surveyed the situation. As the shots stopped, we saw police cars coming from both directions. The shots had seemed to come from behind the home I was going to visit. The police cars met in the middle of the block and both slammed on their brakes by our vehicles. Their windows were down. The cop in the car closest to us identified us quickly and asked Tom if he knew where the shots had come from. Tom told him what he knew and they peeled out, circling the block. Tom told me I would be safer in the house, so I ran to the already opened front door where the patient was anxiously waiting for me.

She pulled me inside and said, "Thank God you are okay. They have been shooting around here all day."

In the home I was a little shook up, but I collected myself enough to do a superb assessment. I didn't hurry, maybe because I didn't want to go back outside. Then I grew concerned for Tom and decided to wrap things up so that we could get out of there.

I worked quickly, but was careful and deliberate enough to ensure that everything was covered with the patient and also that I gave her plenty of time to get answers to all of her questions. As I was doing this, she said, "Miss Tia, you need to stop worrying about me and just get in your car and get the hell out of here."

I appreciated that. We hugged and I almost flew out the door, hurrying to Lola and heading for home. On the way, Tom texted me and said that there had been fifteen shots and the police were still looking for the shooters. Tom and I always got along great, but it seemed like there was always a lot of action whenever I called him.

There was, however, one time when I had called Tom and the patient visit went perfectly. The streets were clear and there had been absolutely no activity. I left the home to find him looking at the back of Lola. I walked up to Tom to see that he was fiddling with my license plates.

"Look at this," he said as I walked up. "Someone tried to rip off your license."

I looked at it. All that was left of my now-bent Washington Redskins license plate read "Skins."

"That's a shame," he said, shaking his head.

I told Tom that I'd had those license plates for over eight years without a problem, but even on an uneventful day and a perfect patient visit, there had been this small issue. I couldn't really blame Tom, though. The truth is that I knew that this damage could have occurred in front of my own home. It hadn't necessarily happened during work.

What I did learn is that Tom was always on the ball. He didn't miss *anything*.

CHAPTER 10

My Dad Doesn't Believe in Heaven, So There

As I was getting ready for work one morning, I decided to get dressed up a little more than usual. I was going to a restaurant for a meeting with a family and their friends. I looked forward to this and to the fact that I would be going to a different part of the city today, so I headed out, looking sharp.

I was taking care of a dying man who was having a lot of mental issues, which is common. The doctor had prescribed medication that would address these issues. The family was very religious and there was a concern among his friends. They did not want him to put anything in his body that would in any way alter his thinking. The patient's daughter was in favor of the medications, but all of his friends and fellow churchgoers were against them, so my meeting with them at the restaurant was to discuss this situation.

The patient had a very nice home and it was clear that the daughter was taking great care of her father. A parade of older visitors was there daily. They were all very supportive of the daughter, but for religious reasons, they had a major problem with the medications prescribed for his mental health. I had talked extensively with the daughter the day before, and she assigned me the task of convincing them all that her father needed the medication.

I pulled up to the restaurant and went inside for some breakfast. I entered the reserved room and looked around. There were a dozen faces there, most of which I recognized as visitors to the patient's home. They were all very polite and obviously knew one another well. We ordered and ate a fine breakfast without any discussion of the issue. I sat next to the daughter so that we could plot our strategy a bit while everyone enjoyed their breakfast.

She wished me good luck and I stood up, thinking that I really didn't have a lot of time to get this accomplished. I had a lot of patients to visit. I looked around to study the faces of the patient's ten religious friends and thanked them all for showing up.

I told them that sometimes when people are dying, the pain medicines are not the only tools that are employed to make patients as comfortable as possible. I explained that in the case of their friend, he had been prescribed medication that would calm him down and address some of the mental issues that he was struggling with. I went on to tell them that this was common and that the daughter and I would like to proceed with giving him this medication, but we wanted them in agreement. I invited them to ask me any questions they had.

They all spoke at once. Then there was silence. And then half of them spoke at once again, so I interrupted and suggested we go around the table, taking turns to hear their concerns. As we went around the table, each friend offered a different version of how these drugs were against their religious beliefs and how they could not support the idea of their friend taking them.

The daughter looked at me and gave me a look that said, "What the hell are you going to say now?"

I stood up again and thanked them for their thoughts. I told them that I was truly impressed at how much they cared for their friend. I then suggested that perhaps many people they knew, including other family members, were taking a variety of drugs that affect the mind in a positive way and that these drugs enable people to function in their daily lives. Most of them politely shook their heads, indicating that they were not aware of this taking place in their circle.

So then I asked them if they had heard of any of a list of medications I rattled off and if any of their friends and family were perhaps taking them. I recited the names of about ten common drugs and they all started looking at one another. I knew what they were thinking. They were familiar with these drug names and they did, indeed, know people who were taking them.

A few of them politely started up the basic religious argument again. The daughter saw this and jumped up from her seat and blurted out, "My dad does not believe in heaven."

What the hell, I thought. *Why did she say that to a room full of his religious friends?* There was silence, total silence. I'm not sure what she was trying to do with this remark, but she seemed to have scared the hell out of the group.

I acted as if she hadn't said anything, and then I asked the group if they had any specific questions about the medicines. One of the ladies started talking about some of her friends who were taking one of the medicines I had mentioned. Then a buzz started. It seemed that the group was in the process of realizing that perhaps there were a lot more of these medications out there than they all had previously thought.

The daughter looked at me with supportive eyes. I backed off a little and they talked amongst themselves for a short time, then fell silent. One of the women at the other end of the table said, "Could we take some of these pills ourselves to see what they do?"

At this point I was thinking, *this is wild*. As surprising and strange as her comment had been, I was feeling good. We were almost over the goal line. "Sure you can," I told them. "I will get some bottles and pass them around the table. Right after that, I will lose my nursing license and so will the doctor who prescribed them." I realized that I had come across as a smartass, so I grew more serious.

"I will tell you what I know about each medicine generally and provide you with specific reading materials that will give you a complete explanation. I cannot tell you what medicines we might give your friend or whether we give him any medicine at all," I said. "If I was taking care of any you, I am sure this would be what you would want also." I went on to explain that this was private information and that perhaps the family may or may not want to share it with them. I hadn't closed the sale yet, but I went for and "assumed sale." I thanked them for being so caring of their friend and said that we would proceed with whatever the doctor had ordered and the family supported. They seemed fine with that.

By now it seemed to me that our breakfast meeting had achieved its purpose and the task at hand had been completed. I got up to leave and almost all of them came up to me and shook my hand or hugged me. This was very nice. They were satisfied, and they also then knew that others in their family and circle of friends were taking medications that they had previously thought were against their religious beliefs—or they knew it all along but none of them had talked about it. I left them to deal with that.

There was also the issue of the daughter telling this formidable group of religious friends that her father does not believe in heaven. I think they just put that out of their minds. Discussing the use of medications with regard to religious beliefs had been difficult enough. But theological debates on the existence of heaven—this was just too much for them.

The daughter walked me out and thanked me the whole way. I was glad to be of assistance and thought, *good luck to you on the not-believing-in-heaven thing*.

CHAPTER 11

I Took My Dying Dad's Pills for My Toothache

One day I needed to go by a home to address a situation where a patient's daughter had been taking care of her father, but not in a perfect way. I had been there a few days earlier, and the daughter had been having trouble accounting for all the meds. I never accuse anyone of any illegal activity, but it's my job to make sure that every pill or drop of medicine is accounted for.

The daughter was being paid by the state to take care of her father—a not-uncommon practice. When I first heard of this type of arrangement, I thought that it was a little weird that someone would want to be paid to take care of a family member. The rationale is that this helps keep the patient in the home and provides income to the family caregiver—very helpful if they had quit a job.

Almost always, this arrangement works well, but sometimes the person taking care of the patient is nowhere to be found or does not do a perfect job. In this particular case, a social worker had been concerned that the patient's daughter may not have been performing her duties as required.

The daughter had called in earlier in the week to order some additional medicine and asked if she could get some new medical supplies also. I went by the home the next day to visit with the daughter. She wasn't there, but she arrived a few minutes later. I told her that I needed to do an inventory on the medications. She told me that they were all accounted for and that she had control of the situation. I replied that it was my job to account for the pills and that this had to happen.

She opened up a giant white purse and brought out what was left of the medications. I looked at them quickly and could see that the medications were still almost all there. I am different than some people who have a "gotcha" attitude. I am happy when things are not messed up. I asked her why she had not been giving the pills to her father. She told me that he'd told her he wasn't in any pain, so she hadn't given them to him.

I said okay, thanked her, and went into the room to see the patient. It was clear that he wasn't being cared for. I found soiled, urine-soaked sheets, probably a couple of days old. I cleaned him up and changed the bedding. I spoke to him about all of his issues and the pain. It turned out that the daughter was right about the pain situation, but I was angry about the lack of care.

I went back into the living room to meet with the daughter. The pills were on the coffee table. I told her that she had been correct that her father did not seem to be in any pain. While we talked, I counted the pills and found only one missing.

I asked her why there was only one pill missing and she said, "I had a toothache, so I took one myself."

I hesitated a minute and then replied that she should not have done that, and that since her father wasn't in any pain, I was going to flush the pills down the toilet. She gave me a look that seemed to acknowledge I was on to her and it was over.

Feeling the situation was futile, I decided not to talk to her about her calling in for more pills. I determine that we needed a bigger solution. I called her older brother who has "power of attorney" for the patient. I asked him if we could meet and make some changes in his father's care.

We met the next day at the home and the daughter was not there. In fact, she hadn't been there since I had talked to her last. I told him the whole sorry story, and he was embarrassed and mad. He said he had another sister and he was confident she would do a great job, so we agreed to make the change.

Changing caregivers worked out very well for the patient. The new sister turned out to be a blessing for the situation. From then on, the father was clean as a whistle and the daughter was always on top of the situation.

CHAPTER 12

How Many Accountants Does It Take to Give a Dying Patient Her Meds?

It was mid-day and I was going to see one of my favorite patients, Phyllis. She was a little bitty woman who had been ill for over twenty years. Her condition had worsened to the point where she did not have long to live. Phyllis had a boyfriend of twenty years who was an accountant. In fact, the boyfriend was an accountant, Phyllis's son was an accountant, and her sister was an accountant. All of them were involved in her care.

Soon after I was assigned the patient, I received a call from Phyllis's physician. I had worked with this doctor before so we knew one another well. He told me that the family was a little difficult to handle and warned me that the boyfriend would challenge me on just about everything. He then reassured me that he knew I could handle him.

My previous meeting with the family had gone well. I met all the players and was impressed with the brainpower that Phyllis had for her care. I thought things would be well taken care of. I went over all the medicines with the team and they all nodded, indicating that they were good to go.

I also had a very good visit with Phyllis that day. She told me how she had been writing letters for all of her family members that each of them could open at a future date for important events. So there was a stack of letters for birthdays, anniversaries, marriages and graduations. I thought this was a truly wonderful and thoughtful idea.

Phyllis was a neat person and I loved talking to her. I asked her why she was all dressed up, and she told me they were headed to synagogue soon to have all the bad spirits removed from her body. I had never heard of such a thing, but hey, it sounded good to me and I told her so.

She then mentioned that she had something silly to ask me. I thought for a moment that this was a first. No one had ever told me they were going to ask me a silly question. *This should be good*, I thought. I told her to go ahead, and added that I would answer the best I could.

She hesitated and then asked me if it would be okay if she drank a little wine and ate some McDonald's food. I laughed a little inside, and then told her that she could have anything she wanted to eat and drink. She went on to describe the specific wine she preferred and the awesome pancakes and oatmeal she has become addicted to from McDonald's. She described the wine and food in great detail and was growing happier and happier as she went on.

Having had success with this first request, she then asked if she could have a few Heinekens once in a while. *You are dying and you are asking me if this is okay?* But I knew she needed my reassurance. I told Phyllis that of course she could have a Heineken once in a while, and that I hoped she enjoyed every bit of it. Knowing how this works, I told her that I would inform the family so they knew she had my blessing. She seemed glad to hear this.

While dietary issues had seemed to cause Phyllis a bit of consternation, it turned out that these were the least of our worries. A few days later, I received a call that there was a concern that the boyfriend and the other accountants had messed up the medicines, so I headed to the house to clear up the situation.

I pulled up to their lovely home and went inside after a very warm greeting at the door from Phyllis's sister. I told them that I wanted to see Phyllis for a second before we went over the meds. Phyllis was doing wonderfully. She thanked me again for improving her diet and for allowing her to have a few drinks. We laughed a little, and I went into the living room for the meeting about the medications.

I had thought that this would take about five minutes or so. Much to my surprise, for the next forty-five minutes or so, I watched the accountants debate why none of them were at fault for the medication mix up. I really didn't care who was to blame; all I wanted to do was fix the problem. They finally stopped and asked me what I thought. I told them that I knew none of them would intentionally do anything to harm Phyllis, so all we needed to do was fix the issue and I would be on my way.

That wasn't good enough. They wanted me to pick out the person who had made the mistake. This must have been an accountant thing. I couldn't tell who had made the error because after about twenty minutes, I had tuned them out. Seeing no end in sight, I switched to a strategy where I would take the blame. I told them that the problem was most likely the way I had used some medical terms, and that combined with my use of military times, that had most likely given them the wrong impression. Then I said, "This was not your fault." I actually knew whose fault it was, but I ain't telling. They all straightened up in their chairs and looked at each other in agreement. They each had that "it wasn't my fault" look on their faces and this was just what they wanted—or needed.

Finally, I went over the medication instructions in exactly the same way that I had the first time. The boyfriend was reviewing the paper on which I had written this down on the first visit. He glanced at me over the top of his reading glasses. I could tell he knew I knew he blew it, and he seemed relieved that I wasn't calling him out.

It was cool. He was happy. It is my job to take care of all of the family, even the boyfriend who accidently gave the patient the wrong medicine.

In the visits that followed, the boyfriend called me "The General." He listened better and did a solid job. We had our secret that we never talked about. I told him that my grandfather also calls me "The General."

Encounters like these remind me of one of the many things I like about my job: helping the family and patient can come in all forms. I had helped the patient and saved the accountant's pride. So how many accountants does it take to give a patient her medicine? Just one now. It's a good thing there were no light bulbs to screw in.

CHAPTER 13

I Hate White People

One morning I got up a little earlier than usual because I had a lot of visits scheduled for the day. While I was making sure my two kitties, Riggins (named after John Riggins, the famous Washington Redskins football player) and Muffin, were set for the day with food and water, I received a phone call. It was Shana, one of my patients, and she very calmly told me that someone had stolen her wheelchair. After asking her if she was okay, I asked for details on how it had happened. I was thinking she'd been out somewhere and that thieves had yanked her out of the wheelchair and run off with it. Instead, she told me that someone took it from her home. I asked her how that could have happened, and she said that someone had broken into her home and stolen it. After she said that she had looked everywhere for it, I told her I would make a few calls to see what I could do. While it's disappointing to think that someone would steal a dying person's wheelchair, this was not an unusual call for the area I work in, so I called it in for the service to handle.

My first in-person call that day was with a very special lady, Maggie. She had no family and only a few friends and she lived alone. I always looked forward to visiting with Maggie because her presence was calming. She was very quiet-spoken and listened a lot more than she spoke. While I tried to draw Maggie out and get to know her better, she always kept firing questions at me about my life. I often wished I could be more like her. She knew quite a bit more about me than I could get from her about herself. We did talk at length about all the issues in the neighborhood.

Maggie told me that I always smelled great and that I was a very attractive young woman. She was mostly curious why I had chosen to do the work I was doing. I buy gifts for my patients from time to time, mostly their favorite food, and I thanked her by giving her a bottle of the perfume I use. She was surprised and very grateful.

I arrived at her home, which was very small and quite old. As with many of the homes I visited, I could see that she did her best to keep her home neat and clean. She pulled weeds and had a man in the neighborhood keep the home painted, even though the boards on the house were crooked and some were about to fall off.

I went inside and Maggie gave me her usual warm and soft greeting. I asked her how she was doing and she said that she was okay, but she told me that she had something she had been struggling with. I replied that she should just let it rip. Still troubled, she said that it was something that she couldn't tell me. *Now I have to know*, I thought. Then her eyes started to fill with tears.

She turned away and walked into the middle of the living room/dining room area which had a bed in it. She turned around and faced me and said, "Tia, I hate white people."

Now what do I say? I thought. *Did she mean she hates me, and if so, should I leave?* I knew I wasn't going to leave, because I knew in my heart that she didn't hate me. Even if she did, I still had to do my job. I didn't know what to say, so I said, "That's okay." I don't know what the hell that meant, but at least there wasn't any of that damned silence.

Then she told me that, of course, she didn't hate me, but she was struggling because all of her life she and her friends had always talked about how they hated the white people. She went on to say that until she met me, she had never really known any white people. She said that all of this had confused and troubled her. By this point in our conversation, I was just glad that Maggie didn't hate me. I wasn't really caring about the rest of the white people at the time. They were on their own. She was waiting for me to say something but I wasn't ready, so I told her that I thought it was a good thing that she realized that maybe she should be a little more open to giving all people a chance.

That didn't sound so good when it got out there, but she could tell I wasn't offended.

Then she asked me to sit on the couch with her. She told me that when she had first met me, she was disappointed that I was white, but she immediately could tell I was a take-charge person who knew what I was doing. She felt she had no choice but to put up with me. She said she was most impressed that I seemed so comfortable in the area and in her home.

Maggie said her change of heart had come when we were in the middle of a conversation and she realized that I did not have to be working in her neighborhood—that I wanted to—and also that I was not faking it. She said that this was a hard thing to come to grips with. "All that hate I held inside for years just dragged me down and wasted my time," she said. "I just had to tell you this because I couldn't tell anybody else."

"Well, this is a good day," I said. "I'm happy that you got this off your chest."

I conducted my normal assessment and went over the meds. I wanted to stay, but it had been a very busy day and there were more visits on my schedule. I stayed a few extra minutes and then got up to go. We had always hugged when I left, but it occurred to me that this day's hug was probably the most genuine that she had ever given me. Then she said in her low voice, "I love you, Tia."

I broke the hug and stepped back about a foot, grabbed both her hands, looked her in the eyes and told her that I loved her, too.

That day weighed heavily on me. I was happy but exhausted, mostly from having to think of appropriate and sincere responses for such a difficult conversation. I knew the patient was relieved and happy, so I told myself to just focus on that.

My encounter with Maggie made me think about one of our African-American nurses who went into an almost all-white, wealthier neighborhood recently. She told me that she thought the call had gone very well, but when she got back to the office, she found that the family had called the service and said that they really would prefer to have a white nurse.

When she had told me about this, we'd both laughed, but I was also embarrassed for our whole race. Nurses hear and see much. The good thing is that we take care of one another and remain professional.

I made a few other calls that day that went fine, and I had one more call to make before heading home for some Monday night football. John came with me for the call. It was in an apartment building, and John's concern was that there might be drug dealing going on in the houses next door and across the street.

John does all that "alleged" talk and never officially accuses anybody of anything. But when he tells me about "alleged" activity, I know he is seeing it happen. The other issue was that while it was an apartment building, in order to get outside, the top-floor residents had to come down the steps from their apartment and walk through my patient's kitchen.

On previous visits, when I would be talking to a family member of the patient, someone would come down the stairs that even the family didn't know. This was weird for all of us! I had been making an extra call to this patient because they said that someone had stolen their drugs again. Hospice nurses do not mess around with drugs—we account for every pill.

The first time the patient's medications were stolen we replaced them because the patient needed the drugs and we had no reason to believe they were not telling the truth. On this particular visit, however, I was called to the house because they said on the phone that they had some information for me about the drugs. That's all the entire message said.

So I arrived, looking around just to make sure John was there, and knocked on the apartment door. I went inside and was greeted by the patient's daughter, Wanda. We had always gotten along very well and had many lively conversations—until the first batch of drugs were missing. After that, our relationship had become more serious and somewhat strained.

But on this visit Wanda had returned to her old self, all cheery and such. It was clear that she was busting to tell me something.

I had put on my serious face. "What's going on?" I asked.

She was excited. "Tia you won't believe it! We set up a camera in the kitchen and caught Milly taking the drugs off the counter." Milly was her neighbor who lived upstairs.

"That's so cool!" I said.

Wanda went on to explain that she had called the building's landlord and he had asked Milly to leave the premises—permanently. I wondered why they did not call the police—along with wondering whether I was the only person in the world who didn't seem to have a security camera lying around that I could just put up in my kitchen.

Wanda was happy and invited me in to see the video, and this made me happy, too. Who wouldn't want to see that? I went into the living room and there was a tangle of wires, looking like black spaghetti, all connected to a 1980s VCR that fed into the TV. They fired it up and were just as excited as the first time they viewed it, I'm sure. I was excited, too!

Wanda was pleased because she knew I had lost a little trust in her once the drugs went missing, and I was happy for the same reason. We kind of hugged and jumped up and down together at the same time and then watched the video three more times. Each time was like the first.

She grabbed me and walked me into the kitchen, proudly showing me the drugs that had been recovered. Wanda's family had sent their cousin to Milly's home to deal with her and reclaim the drugs. Maybe I don't want to meet that cousin.

As fun as this was, I reminded myself of my priority and broke away to take care of the patient. I found myself in a good mood that rubbed off on the patient.

I said my goodbyes, making sure Wanda knew our relationship had been set right. I found myself surprised that this was so important to her, and couldn't help but reflect on how cool that was.

Now, I thought, *if the Redskins can pull out a victory tonight, I will have a perfect day!*

CHAPTER 14
Nature Calls

After I had been on the job for some time, I decided to sit down and review the determining factors that I used to make up my mind on whether or not to utilize our security personnel. I was utilizing security more than those I followed and wanted to be prepared in case I was ever asked. I love my job and I want to conduct my business thoroughly, and at times I need the security to do that. Below is my list of twenty-nine reasons that justify my use of security:

1. ***Dogs running loose around patient's home or the patient has dogs that are unattended.*** There is a patient whose dogs were supposed to be penned up. The dogs had come out three times during my visit—after we had asked them twice to restrain the dogs. These dogs are usually pit bulls or Rottweilers. John came close to shooting them for our safety. These animals do not like strangers in their home and many times are protective of the patient. Perhaps, as some people believe, dogs can sense when a patient is sick and dying and may blame a stranger for this condition. While visiting a patient on Cleveland Street, we witnessed a man beating his dog with a chain in the next-door neighbor's yard. All we could do was watch. I've had several instances of this kind, and if I was alone, I would most

likely have to leave immediately. With John present to handle this type of incident, I can do my work.

2. ***Activity outside with people yelling and fighting.*** While seeing a patient on Benton Street, John and I witnessed a man beating his girlfriend with his fists in their car for forty-five minutes. John called the police and all we could do was watch. The police pulled up, looked in the car, asked a few questions and left. The couple never even got out of the car. We see a lot of fighting and arguing while making patient visits. The concern is that walking right by these incidents to get into the patient's home could be dangerous. They could attack me or possibly even take a shot. John's presence enables me to get inside the home safely.

3. ***Information that the patient, family and neighbors tell me regarding security issues in the area.*** On State Street, the patient's caregiver told me that the neighbor's house had been shot up the night before as a result of drug activity. Over half of my patients have told me about recent crimes in their neighborhoods, thus the safety issue isn't merely confined to the patient's home. Of course, I must not only drive to the patient's home, I must also drive to the next patient or home. In the meantime, I may need to eat or get something to drink. There is no place in these neighborhoods where I can safely go to do this. For example, once I stopped at a Subway sandwich shop in the neighborhood. This store featured bulletproof glass at the counter, people hanging out in the store yelling things at me (basically that I didn't belong in their neighborhood). I did, however, learn some new combinations of foul language words.

4. ***Domino's doesn't deliver to most of the ZIP codes I visit.*** Just as Subway will locate in an area and equip its stores with bulletproof glass, some large companies have examined the statistics and the personal experiences of their employees and determined that, from a risk-management perspective, it is simply not safe to do business in these neighborhoods, even if they might want to.

5. ***No roadside assistance.*** Roadside services generally will not go into the areas I serve. If I would have car trouble, for example, a flat tire, a breakdown, or keys locked in the car, I would quickly be in trouble if alone.

6. ***Crime on the street, shootings all hours of the day and night.*** Families talk freely of daily crimes in their neighborhoods. They are

concerned for their safety and often mine. One example of this occurred on Washington Street. The patient's daughter is a police officer. She would wait on her mom's porch with her gun to ensure that I remained safe. Other family members have told me they are armed and will look out for my safety while I am at their home.

7. ***Crime activity at the patient's home.*** On Market Street, my patient's family told me that family members were selling drugs in front of the house during my visit. On another day, John observed the alleged sales transactions during my visit. In addition, drugs were allegedly being sold across the street. The family told me they watched one of their family members hand over drugs, take the money in return, and provide the buyer with a fist bump.

8. ***Time for business.*** John had to get his gun out and ready during one of my visits. While at a visit on Benton Street, John had to unholster his gun and place it on his lap as a result of gangs gathering in the front of the houses on both sides of the street while I was in the home. John was concerned that bad things were about to happen. While I am in a house, I have no idea what may be going on outside. If events outside the house get bad enough, John can call me and tell me to stay inside until things settle down. This has happened before. I can also call John to ask him to come inside for his own safety if there is any kind of danger. I have done that on a couple of occasions also.

9. ***Bicycle guards.*** On Washington and Wabash Streets, kids on bikes ride up and down the streets when I arrive to let the drug dealers know the "popo" has arrived. These are the spotters for the gangs, so we know that the gang members are active in the area. Active gangs can mean danger if we don't mind our own business. This information was told to me by my patients' families.

10. ***Abandoned houses.*** About one fourth of the homes in some of the communities I visit are vacant. Several of these have activity outside of them. The area police have told me this activity is likely drug sales or drug usage. Any normal person would feel uncomfortable parking and walking by this type of activity—and for good reason. Having security enables me to navigate these types of danger-fraught obstacle courses without as much fear.

11. ***Trash removal is not widespread.*** In a few areas, there are White Castle boxes and Colt 45 cans lying about. There are couches and

sometimes TVs in the streets. None of that represents a safety issue. The problem is the boards with nails sticking up and metal objects in the road that have fallen off of the metal scrappers' trucks. I often have to dodge a lot of debris when driving through the areas. I hit objects twice and got flat tires. I had to call John to come out and change my tire before something bad happened. He arrived and changed the tire immediately, well before roadside ever showed up. Seconds count when left vulnerable in these neighborhoods.

12. ***Business security.*** Like many of the businesses in the area, Walgreens has reserved parking in front of their stores for the police. In addition, most of the other shops and businesses in the area employ security guards in their stores. To me, this is a measurable sign of ongoing concern for the likelihood of crimes being committed.

13. ***Weapons and convicts in the homes.*** I am comfortable saying that I think there are weapons in some of the patients' homes I visit. This is part of their way of life, but the fact is, guns are there when I am there. There is the potential that one "bad son" or friend who has been in trouble using weapons in the past may be present. These persons regularly wander through the homes while I conduct my patient visits. I do know for a fact that I have been in the presence of convicted felons and others who have done jail time for various crimes. One of my patients was actually convicted of murder. In another situation, I called the prison to see if they could release a son to come home to see his dying mother. It is wise to have security in these situations.

14. ***Family discord.*** Relatives who are not welcome sometimes arrive during my visits. One example of this occurred when I had a patient whose girlfriend did not get along with the patient's daughters. The girlfriend had knives and a machete in the apartment. She told me that if one of his daughters showed up, she would "take care of them." The day before my visit, the girlfriend told one of our staff members that she had chased the patient's brother out of the apartment with the machete. So what if the brother returns or the patient's daughter shows up during my visit? I would not like to be in the vicinity of potential hand-to-hand combat, and having security reduces the risk.

15. ***What are you doing here?*** I myself have been pulled over three times by the police. They would ask me what I was doing in the neighborhood. They know it's not safe for me to be the neighborhood alone. On

one occasion I was traveling unescorted. An officer was sitting in an alley across from my patient's house and asked me what I was doing there. After explaining that I was there to see a patient, he said that he would stay there during my visit. He went on to tell me that I should never be there unaccompanied.

16. ***I use my instincts.*** On both occasions when I left during a visit without security and later took security with me the next time, my instincts were right. During the first instance, the patient's son was escalating with me and threatening me. I pretended I had a call from a patient and told him I had to go to see a patient in crisis. I fabricated this excuse to get out of the building. He followed me out of the apartment yelling, "You will come back here and see my mother now!" I continued to walk to my car and told him I would call him and schedule another appointment. He was a different person when I returned with security.

    On another occasion, I had gone to see a new patient. During the visit, the son stood up and yelled and pointed his finger in my face because he didn't think the information I was telling him about his mother's disease process was correct. He reminded me that I was not a doctor. I tried to explain that I had been in constant contact with the doctor and that at any time he could speak to the doctor if he didn't trust what I was saying. This just made him even more angry. Families of patients get mad. They may be going through the toughest time of *their* lives. Usually, they eventually calm down, but it seems that some of these people are bullies, especially when it comes to dealing with women. I can take a great deal, but when it keeps me from giving first-class care, or when I truly fear for my life, it makes sense to have security present to calm them down.

17. ***Family locks up narcotics. Why?*** In some cases, we lock up the drugs when the family has a concern that they will be misused. This is a warning sign. The family may have the concern—from past experience—that there could potentially be an issue. Also, local pharmacies do not deliver in some of my areas. This is another warning sign. There is a perception that we carry drugs. We would be a target.

18. ***Retaliation.*** We all see the number of crimes that take place in my territory, which is the third-largest crime area in the country. Those who live there know that after a crime comes retaliation. Thus anyone working there needs to maintain security following recent, almost daily,

crimes. On Delmar, directly across the street from my patient's apartment, there was a drive-by shooting in May around two o'clock in the afternoon. Two girls were shot. That night, someone was killed at the same location. On my next nursing visit the following week, there were two police officers in the parking lot of my patient's residence due to another drive-by shooting that afternoon.

19. ***Police don't pull over cars unless they have another officer with them.*** Police do not patrol without their own protection. In the neighborhoods I serve, almost all police cars have two officers. They also generally do not pull over and get out of their patrol cars until another car arrives. Just like me, the police who have a wealth of knowledge know that they need backup to do their job safely in this area. The number one job of the police is to save themselves first, then the citizens. The number one job of my security is to save Tia first, then themselves. This is one of the reasons that John, Tom and Patrick do not get involved in other criminal activity in the area, because that would distract them from protecting me or another nurse. The other reason they don't get involved is that they want to make it visible within the community that they are only concerned with keeping me safe and not with anyone else's business—or criminal—activity. Our hope is to be left alone to do our thing, and we will do the same for any who notice our presence. I have seen this work many times. Our security detail does have reporting responsibilities and this does take place.

20. ***Ambulances do not go into the area without police protection.*** Paramedics going into the neighborhoods that I visit require protection as a result of a history of crimes committed against them. If paramedics need police escort, then I need security as well.

21. ***GPS is not always correct.*** Having GPS can be helpful but does not guarantee safety. Barricades don't show up on GPS. In addition, some of the metal scrappers have found out that the street signs have value. It is an unfortunate reality that the metal scrappers often take down the street signs and scrap them for some quick cash. The result is that it can be hard to find your way around in the neighborhood. It is also not an ideal place to "look lost" or to stop and ask for directions.

22. ***Security has deterred crime from happening.*** Having John's, Patrick's and Tom's presence has resulted in people backing off and leaving the area when there has been a potential incident. I can think of several situations where trouble was averted as a result of my security being pre-

sent. In addition, the local teens can time the length I am in the house and without security could break into my car or rob me when I am leaving, and I would be helpless.

23. **Concrete barriers.** There are concrete bollards that serve as barriers in the streets, so there is only one way in and one way out in some situations. If you needed to get out quickly, you may not be able to do so. Furthermore, the number of barriers has been increasing. Security can cover for me as I am turning around at these barriers.

24. **Curbside service.** One of my hospice patients was homeless, so I met her on the street and she had a horrible wound that was oozing from her chest. Her t-shirt was saturated with drainage. With John's help, we improvised a makeshift curtain, creating a privacy area at the back of his Tahoe, and I was able to clean the wound and apply new dressing. What if John had not been there? Because he was there, I was able to take care of business and provide the patient with privacy.

25. **Climate.** In the winter, they do not clear the snow from the sidewalks and streets in a timely fashion. I have a two-wheel-drive vehicle. It is very easy for me or any caregiver to get stuck in the snow while driving to or parking at a patient's home. It would be a long walk in the snow to get anywhere I would feel safe.

26. **Shots fired.** Fifteen shots were fired during one of my visits behind the patient's home. Two police officers arrived and asked John if he saw where the shots had come from. Gunfire is routinely heard in my area and this is a consideration for the use of security.

27. **"I can't get out."** Bars on windows and doors locked from the inside with a key are an issue. In many instances, it is as hard for me to get out of a house as it was to get in. Many of my clients, as a result of their own security needs, secure just as much from the inside as the outside. I always make sure I have a way out. This is sometimes very difficult in these homes. That is why I need to be in phone contact with security when I am in the home. What if the person holding the key to the front door decides they like my company? In these situations, I need to be able to summon security.

28. **Crime reports.** One of the most important factors for determining the use of security is crime reports from my area. These are the streets I drive up and down every day. Following are a few examples from a recent report found on spotcrime.com:

June 15-Shooting in the 2300 block of Cole Street.

June 22-Shooting on Warren Avenue as a woman was shot in the face, shoulder and head. The woman died.

June 26-A man was shot to death on Benton Street off 24th at 1:45 in the afternoon. This incident happened fifteen minutes before I drove down Benton to see a patient on 23rd Street.

July 6-Shooting during the afternoon.

These are just some of the crimes over a relatively short period of time. I keep an eye on the reports on a regular basis as I am planning my future visits. This helps me determine if I need security and also helps me to plan the route I take to each of my calls.

29. **Nature calls.** I have a policy of not using the restrooms of my patients. I have been in many of them to get things for the patients. Most are great, many cleaner than my own, but to me their bathrooms are their personal space. So imagine you are in the center of the territory described above. Now imagine that it is a very hot day, and you have continually been drinking gallons of water for the past four hours. Remember that time in your life when you really, *really* had to go to the bathroom. Holding it is not an option. Here are your choices: 1) You can pee in your pants; or 2) you can go to a gas station where you may be taking your life in your hands. This was a one-time occurrence, but I don't know what would have happened if I had not had John with me. The issue was that I couldn't leave the territory because I had other patients to see. Here is what transpired. John and I had several visits back to back on one of the hottest days of the year. None of the homes had air conditioning and I was slamming down the water to stay cool. As I had just completed a visit, I called John from inside the home and told him I needed to get to a restroom. Once out of the house, I ran to my car. John could tell by my tone on the phone that this was a serious situation. He sprang into action. John immediately pulled out in front of me and I followed him. Normally he always follows me. We shot down the road, rolling the stop signs. It seemed like an eternity, but we finally pulled in to the Gas Station Store. I jumped out of the car and John got out of his vehicle. I asked John why he was getting out and he replied that there was no way he would let me go in the by myself.

While I was happy to be there, I noticed the bulletproof glass on the cashier's cage, the people hanging around and all the trash inside and outside the building. It was filthy.

So then I went into the restroom as I saw out of the side of my eye everyone watching us. They had absolutely no idea what was going on.

The restroom was disgusting. The walls, which had originally been white, were now mostly a brown-yellowish color from all the years of smoke and filth. Graffiti and handprints marred the walls and wet trash rotted on the floor. I decided at that moment to throw away my shoes when I escaped this place. The restroom's faucet was dripping and there was a crust of thick, grimy "something" on the sink. There was no soap and no paper towels; no toilet lid or toilet paper. The real challenge was to do my business without touching anything. I flushed the toilet with one of my shoes and opened the door with the other shoe. I came out of the toilet and there was John standing right outside the bathroom door. He didn't say a word.

I murmured that I would pee by a tree before I would go to one of these places again. All of the individuals hanging around the station still looked as if they were just wondering who the hell we were. So there I was, headed back to my patients after soaking as much of my body as possible with the bottle of germ killer I keep in my car.

Let's just say that I would most likely have peed myself if I had not had security that day. Having security allowed me to take care of my personal business and get back on the job.

CHAPTER 15

August 2014: The Whole World Watches as Ferguson, Missouri Erupts

On August 8, 2014, a young black man named Michael Brown was shot by a white police officer in Ferguson, Missouri. There was an immediate and lasting reaction from the community, which is about seventy percent African American. Protests, rioting and looting broke out, and the police and military responded with force.

This historic event involved tear gas, Molotov cocktails, looting, shots fired, buildings burned, bottles of urine, gas masks, state police, the National Guard, military vehicles, rubber bullets, riot gear, the president, the attorney general, Jesse Jackson, Al Sharpton, the New Black Panther Party, the governor, ABC, CBS, NBC, CNN, FOX, Al Jazeera, and all the talk radio stations and news internet sites

Once the news broke, these events consumed the lives of everyone in the area, including me. We were all glued to the TVs, computers, smartphones, newspapers and radios. The story quickly went international and even the president and attorney general addressed the situation as national figures converged on St. Louis.

My main territory is adjacent to Ferguson and from time to time I see patients there. My boss was very concerned for all of her employees, including me.

We were basically told not to venture into any unsafe conditions as the events were unfolding. "Unsafe" is a relative term to me, as most days I am in a relatively unsafe environment. I also had my security dude who was working double shifts. John would take care of me and others during the day and served as part of the SWAT activities at night. Having him around during this time was reassuring because he had a good deal of insight into what was really happening. He couldn't tell me everything, but his knowledge and experience were extremely helpful.

I kept rockin' in my territory. My patients had to be seen. I was staying up late every night glued to the TV. I was also listening to the radio in my car all day. Like everyone else in the St. Louis area, I was a zombie.

The whole situation seemed surreal. It seemed almost unbelievable that Ferguson had been international news for several weeks. The number of news reporters and media people was amazing. I can remember them saying a few times as the media was reporting on the crowd size that there were more reporters than protesters.

I was tired, scared, sad and disappointed all at the same time as I began making my patient visits the first day.

When someone is dying, as all of my patients are, you build relationships fast. They get to know me lightning-fast because they are so open with me, and I get to know them just as quickly. Some dying people feel they have nothing to lose by what they say. They do not hold back. As a result, they are blunt. Their frankness brings the same out in me. We talk as candid friends.

I sometimes take care of some patients for only one day and then they pass away. Others I have taken care of for over a year. I get close to my patients and their families, so they know me pretty well. At some point, we have discussed race relations. My patients and their families know I am not a prejudiced person. They have told me that. They also know that I would not be doing the job I do if I was. I also think they want to know what I think because I am white. As a result of my relationships, I had no concern about showing up for my job every day under the extreme circumstances of the death of the young man and the coinciding protests.

Most of my patients initially seemed surprised that I would come and see them with all the danger on the streets. They expressed their concern. They were happy to see me and I was happy to see them.

Did we talk about the shooting and the looting and all the craziness? Hell, yes! Their TVs were on and it was absolutely the only thing they wanted to discuss—except for the St. Louis Cardinals, of course. My patients' medical condition is always the number-one focus of my visit. In fact, I think I improved my care during this period of time and truly made sure all of their needs were met and then some.

The conversations were lively and all over the place. I wanted to hear their opinions. In a way, I was very lucky to get to talk to them daily to hear their insights. I also think they were interested in what I was thinking. I had planned not to bring up any of the issues. If they brought it up, I would then try to steer the conversation back to their thoughts. It was only when they pressed me and I knew their views that I would respond.

Did they hold back because I was white? I hoped not and I don't think so. Was I comfortable answering their questions when asked? Yes, this was no problem. In most cases, the patient and the whole family talked for the entire visit, speaking over one another as we went along. No one could get a word in. I was not surprised at how similar our views were.

Generally, we agreed that a few people can do stupid things such as the looting that detracted and distracted from the peaceful protesting.

We also shared an immediate safety concern as any of us would venture out of our homes and get on the streets. Most of my patients and their families live with the daily fear of what might happen as they leave their homes. That fear was escalated now.

I did have a few awkward situations. One such case happened the day after the first looting. I have had patients who told me they were drug addicts. I have had several patients whose family members told me there were drug transactions in the home, front yard or across the street while I was there.

We always looked the other way since John's responsibility was to protect me. As he explained, he can't protect if he gets involved in illegal activity. So as I walked into the home of one of my patients, I looked around as I always do. On the coffee table was a giant bundle of hair extensions of all sizes, shapes and colors. There were enough for the freshman class of any girls' high school.

I flashed back to the previous night's news as I watched the looters running out of a local beauty shop with arms full of hair extensions. I couldn't help but think about where they had come from. I wasn't sure, and I didn't say anything, of course. This was an isolated case.

During my years in the neighborhood, there was often talk of hot merchandise. One of my patients' sons was admiring my red shoes one day. He was a good son and always seemed very respectable. He soon asked me what size shoes I wore and proceeded to tell me he would hook me up with a snappy pair of new red Converse tennis shoes. At first I used to decline these kinds of offers, but I learned that it is an insult to do so. So on this occasion, I just didn't say anything. This was their way of repaying me for taking care of their dying relative. It may also be an indication that they trust me.

Another time I whipped out my brand new work iPhone and was telling another patient's son about how clumsy I was with these kinds of things. He said he would line me up with a new case. Again, I just thanked him. It may seem weird, but I was thinking that this let him know I was not judging him.

In most cases, when the poorest of the poor want to reward you, it is with lots of thank you's, prayers, great food and—if they trust you—hot merchandise. It is all they have to give. The food is my favorite type of "thank you." I have enjoyed many a great meal.

It sounds crazy, but I think if I ever did accept the offer of merchandise, they would know I did not judge them. I could accept a gift and give it to charity once their family member passed, I thought.

As the days of protesting continued, I was becoming even more exhausted from staying up late every night watching the news. The community situation kept growing worse. and my sources were telling me that guns were being confiscated regularly, shots were being fired nightly, and the National Guard had been brought in to support the Ferguson police, the county police and the state police.

As the tension increased, my patients and their families became increasingly concerned for my safety along with their own. Most of the patients assured me they would understand if I skipped some of their visits, but I was good. I continued to see them on schedule.

Several times, one of the men in the house would tell me that they would look out for me, and I always told them that I appreciated it. They meant it. They had guns and I know they would use them if necessary.

As I drove the streets during these times, there was a discernible difference in the community. There were fewer people on the streets, except for the young men. Violent crimes were taking a short break as the gangs had a temporary truce with one another. We had the Crips, Bloods and Chicago-related gangs in the area. Their usual spotters or mules on bicycles were not on the corners.

It was strange. There were also new roadblocks installed which made it more difficult for me to navigate the streets.

While we were all exhausted from staying up too late, the conversations with the patients and the families remained lively. In general, there was a strong feeling in the community that the police officer needed to be arrested immediately and then convicted. It was also the view of most in the community that young black men in particular were being pulled over far too often and harassed by the white police without cause. In their opinion, this view was supported by the fact that the police department was almost entirely white while the community was seventy percent African American.

My patients and their families wanted justice for the family of the slain son. These same families expressed to me their dissatisfaction with the shooters, looters and those throwing rocks, bottles of water, urine, and Molotov cocktails at the police. It occurred to me that these same individuals were the ones who made their lives difficult on a daily basis. I'm sure they may have held back some of their thoughts with me, but not much.

About five days into the protesting and looting, John and I were making a visit. I was in my red Audi and he followed in the Tahoe. I hadn't given it much thought previously, but I was tremendously relieved and grateful to see that vehicle in my rearview mirror as I drove the streets. For a moment I imagined how it would be if I was alone. When I first got the hospice nursing job, I had made some trips alone. I hadn't wanted people to think I was afraid to travel into the territory by myself. While that reasoning was stupid, part of my thinking at that time was related to the cost of security to the company. They were good about it, but I was still concerned.

It didn't take long for me to realize that I could get killed just to save a few bucks. I also knew that I was actually making money for the company by going places where others might hesitate to go. The positive part was that I knew we were picking up some new customers as the word spread that we do a good job for the patients in the area.

Our company was committed to offer our services to everyone, no matter the location.

I was on edge and tired but always happy to see my patients. When I arrived at the home, Yolanda, the patient's daughter, gave me a big hug as she always did and waved to John in the Tahoe. They lived in a two-family flat in a very rough part of the community.

I entered the home and sat on the couch. The TV was on with full-blast coverage of the protesting. I looked around the really small home, a little more aware that day than most. I was doing a lot more thinking about how it must be for my patients to live in their circumstances. I was sad. It must be frightening as well as disheartening to not have a reasonable-sized home in a safe neighborhood—a place where you can unlock your doors, take the bars off the windows, and sit on your porch—without worrying about getting shot.

Like a lot of the homes, this one was clean and tidy, and the family made the best of their circumstances. Most of the homes do not have air conditioning, but they do have fans. There were a lot of fans everywhere. Like a lot of the other homes I have been in, there were many stacks of stuff and boxes of other things filling the small rooms. There was stuff everywhere.

One reason for my sadness on this day is related to what I have heard and felt over many of my visits. As I get to know many of these families, I sense and sometimes they tell me indirectly, that they are embarrassed by their living conditions. They know I am at least "middle class" and most likely have a nice place to live, and they know I have married parents and a brother who is in a normal situation.

Yolanda's home was definitely rough on the outside. The house next door was condemned and the church across the street boarded up. Yolanda told me that another house across the street is a dope house. She said that she would like to move. When I hear that, as I have from so many others, I have a little brain freeze. Most of them really have no hope of ever moving and they know it.

I just wish they knew that I was not judging them because of where they live. I have never found a way to let them know I don't care about where they live. Of course, I wish they could move and I also wish they would not lose the hope of someday moving.

I asked Yolanda how her mother was doing. Yolanda said her mom was fine and there was nothing new with her mom—meaning there were no medical issues that she was aware of. So I went into the dining room, which was now her mom's bedroom, and conducted my assessment. Her vital signs were all good. Yolanda takes great care of her mother.

I could tell Yolanda wanted to discuss her mom's situation and maybe even visit a little. She spent all her time taking care of her mother. and I was company in a way. We sat on the couch together, and of course, we were watching the TV. They were showing a video from the night before—the looting and aggressive protesting with all the military equipment and police involvement. There were young men and women using car batteries to break the windows out of the storefronts in their own neighborhoods.

One scene showed the store's glass actually being shot out with a pistol. The looters were bringing out merchandise by the armload. Some of the looters had brought their children with them. Cars would pull up, fill up and then leave. Other cars would take their place and do the same. The police stood just across the street but did not do anything to stop the looting. It was weird. Why were they not arresting these individuals?

The TV then went back to the protests, and the scene truly looked like a war zone—heavy equipment everywhere, smoke from the tear gas and blasts of light as the tear gas and smoke canisters were fired off. Rubber bullets were being shot at the protesters, who were throwing bottles of water, bottles of urine, rocks and Molotov cocktails. There were also reports of shots fired.

We both watched all of this without saying a word. The TV went to a commercial and neither I nor Yolanda said anything for a little while. All kinds of thoughts were going around in my head and in hers also, I think.

I could tell Yolanda was really saddened by what she was watching. I wondered if she might also be embarrassed by it. Is this just like my patients' embarrassment of where they live? I truly did not know what to say. I was all screwed up, and I started to cry. I don't cry a lot, and people are sometimes confused about why I cry when I cry. I think Yolanda was reading my mind. She reached over and took my hand and said, "Color doesn't matter." I looked down and there was my white hand inside her black hand. The grip was like a mother uses on a daughter. It felt good and reassuring. Wow! Is she good? I sure didn't know what to say—but she knew what to do and say. This was a master stroke on her part because she cut through everything and made me feel better with just three words. She went on to say that those young punks are out in the streets looting and taking what isn't theirs. That's what I was thinking.

I could tell Yolanda was in deep thought and possibly re-living some of the past in her mind. I'm talking about the really horrible part of history for African Americans during the fight for civil rights. The scenes on TV looked far too similar to those from the earlier years of our country. She got out some photo albums and showed me photos of a time when she had been a licensed practical nurse back in the day. I could tell she was proud of her accomplishments. Somewhat out of the blue she said, "Tia, this race thing is never gonna be over." She then went on to tell me about her nursing career.

At the hospital where she had worked, she was paid less than the white nurses. She wasn't allowed to talk to the doctors face to face when they came on the floor to see the patients. She had to put a quarter in a jar if she talked to the wrong white person. She accepted all of this to ensure she made enough money to take care of her children. I heard all of this had gone on, but I had never met anyone who talked about it with me. Talking to me while seeing things unfolding on TV gave her message even more impact. I felt acutely embarrassed by all the white people who ever did anything negative to an African-American person. I had that feeling wash over me right there in that home on that day, a feeling that will stay with me forever. I had experienced glimpses of it before, but it became more real.

Yolanda told me that one day on the hospital floor in front of other nurses, a white doctor gave her one beautiful big red rose as appreciation for all the hard work she had done in taking great care of all his patients. While it may have seemed a small thing to most, this meant a great deal to Yolanda. She walked on clouds for a few days just feeling damned good about herself, thinking that maybe there was a little hope for good things to come. Even though it was just a rose, for Yolanda, the doctor's kind gesture made up for some of the poor treatment that black nurses were expected to tolerate. It had been a good thing all the way around.

Not so fast. Yolanda went on to explain that this once-in-a-lifetime cool thing went horribly bad. The white nurses weren't happy with her getting the rose. Their jealous minds became preoccupied with plotting a hateful counter-attack, and they soon came up with a plan. The plan was to band together with the story that the white doctor had been making an advance at Yolanda while giving her the rose. As bad people can do if there are enough of them or if they are loud enough, they made their case and had Yolanda moved to the night shift.

Yolanda told me the story to let me know that at that point, and when other similar things had happened, she just kept going. She told me she doesn't have resentment toward white people. She said she realized that it was the times they were living in. I, however, was thinking that those nurses needed their asses kicked, and the doctor needed to be a man and fix the situation.

That day I learned that there were many things going on in Yolanda's mind, yet she kept her eye on the prize, which was her family. She got through it and she keeps getting through it.

How eye-opening that day with Yolanda was for me! I realized how little I know about this whole situation, but I now know more than I did before I walked into Yolanda's home that day.

Then came a visitor. Yolanda's eyes lighted up. Some of the sadness went out of them. She stood up and perked up. It was her grandson. He was looking very proud and told her that he had just passed the test and earned his real estate license. Yolanda said, "Hey, don't forget your grandma when you start making all the big bucks." *Now* there was some happiness going on in the house.

Yolanda introduced me to him. "Joseph, this is Tia," she said.

He said, "Nice to meet you, ma'am."

"You can call me Tia," I smiled.

"Okay, ma'am," he said, smiling back.

When young men get around their mom or grandmother, there is a lot of "yes ma'am, no ma'am, and thank you, ma'am" that goes on. Usually the children in the house are directed to call me "Miss Tia, which makes me feel old, but it is kind of cool.

I checked again on the patient and ensured all the medications were in order, and Yolanda and I reviewed all the caregiving issues, and then I was on my way out the door.

I stepped outside, pleased that the visit from the grandson gave Yolanda some much-needed happiness. I was thinking that hospice nurses really do take care of the family and not just the patient. I was also thinking that maybe Yolanda was taking care of me, too. This thought eased my troubled and racing brain.

As the protesting continued across the area, a great sense of exhaustion also continued for me and the families. Outsiders were drawn from near and far to Ferguson, and in some cases they were helpful. In other cases, they simply made things worse.

Several non-Ferguson residents were arrested during the protest. Jesse Jackson, Al Sharpton and the New Black Panthers were there. It was also interesting to see what a tremendously positive impact the local religious leaders were having. There were as many as one hundred of them who regularly placed themselves in between the police and the protesters, actually pointing out criminals who should be arrested within the protester groups.

I've always been very aware of how important churches are in all communities, but it seemed to me that these leaders were getting out in the homes and in the streets more than usual. I regularly listened to my patients and their families talk about all their church-related activities. During the Ferguson unrest, the preachers, priests and ministers sprang into action, and they meant business. In my view, their efforts went a long way to make a bad situation better.

Frankly, the whole situation with Ferguson was surreal. The media from the whole world was covering the events and I was working daily just next to ground zero. The fascinating part was that I was in a cat-bird seat, enabling me to hear all sides as the events unfolded. This changed me.

Some events and conversations reaffirmed my initial views, but daily interactions with the families gave me a new and greater appreciation for all the issues that must be overcome for my families and their community to heal and move forward.

Their struggle is overwhelming. Some have made it and others are on their way, but so many do not see hope. There are, of course, others who unfortunately have no interest in being part of the solution. They are content to continue their destruction and far too often represent the image provided by the media that leads to the negative perceptions of others. These issues are the same in many poor white communities.

At work, the supervisors held meetings to caution us to remain safe at all times. They advised us that if we felt there was too much danger, we should not go. There were protests, crimes, beatings, shootings, vandalism, burnings and lootings. We stayed informed with the newscasts of where the action was taking place, but we knew that it could break out anywhere. Some of our patients could not be moved from the hospital to their homes in Ferguson. It was just too dangerous. The authorities had imposed a curfew, and all of the area schools were closed, as were many businesses, including the twenty or so that were damaged, looted or burned.

John continued to work SWAT at night. The protests spread to a few other locations in the St. Louis area. Ferguson continued to be the lead story on local, national and international news. Eric Holder came to town and pledged a civil rights investigation using forty investigators to gather information. There was still no arrest of the officer.

There was a call by the protesters to remove the white prosecuting attorney, an individual they felt had never worked impartially in an investigation involving police officers. The governor visited the community and various senators popped in for some handshakes and facetime in the media. The National Guard members were sent home for the time being.

The protests continued around the metropolitan St. Louis area, but became less frequent and had smaller crowds. Protesters made attempts to shut down area highways. The primary protests evolved from general anger about the shooting to focus on removing the prosecuting attorney. More witnesses came forward. New videos emerged showing scenes of the site where the shooting had taken place. It was announced that the grand jury would not rule until January, which was months away.

Things slowed down a bit, and we all got some much-needed rest. The gangs returned to committing their crimes. The black-on-black murder rate picked back up. The spotters on bicycles were back out on the corners looking out for the drug dealers and pimps. President Obama mentioned the Ferguson situation in his speech to the United Nations. He was trying to convince the world that we in the U.S. have our own problems as he was giving a speech on global terrorism.

Life in the neighborhoods and on the streets returned to a "new normal," a somewhat uneasy sense of waiting for the grand jury's ruling.

CHAPTER 16
Murder and Baseball

Shootings and murders continued in the city. The protesters, while not as active, continued to protest periodically. They continued to push for the arrest of the officer and the removal of the St. Louis county prosecutor. Over the last weekend of September, there were nine shootings in the city. The police were quick to say that these were not related to the Ferguson situation. *What does that mean?* I wondered. To me it was all part of the situation.

I continued to get my fix every day at a Starbucks. Starbucks was my own personal "Cheers," a place where everybody knows my name. I have a special spot where often I sit and fill in my charting in privacy. It's important to have the privacy because it is illegal for anyone to see what is on my computer. After work some days, we went across the street to a great little restaurant. I have been there many times, often with friends, some of whom are also Starbucks employees. They were my friends also.

Just like at Starbucks, we had all become friends with the workers at the restaurant.

On this day, as a couple of us walked through the front door of the restaurant, we could tell something was wrong. There were somber faces and lots of mumbling. We quickly found out that the head cook had been murdered while getting off a bus on his way home. They said it was a random killing. We were all shocked and saddened. This individual had been special to all of us. He was a quiet young black man who had struggled his whole life to try to stay out of trouble. And he had been making it.

He had just been promoted to head chef at the restaurant. I had spoken to him several times. I remembered the time he explained to me that he was unpopular with the kids he had grown up with because he was trying to make it in what they viewed as the white man's world. He said that his friends repeatedly tried to suck him into their destructive ways. I wondered if they had killed him just because he was making something of himself. I really didn't know who killed him, or why, but I wondered about this anyway.

A few days later, all the patients I had visited were buzzing about baseball. Almost all of my patients are St. Louis Cardinal fans. They love their baseball. The Cardinals were in the playoffs. We had just split with the Dodgers in Los Angeles and the Cardinals were coming home. While I always wear red, I noticed that there was also a lot of red in the homes of my patients. As my visits went on, we all talked about how we would win the game. St. Louis fans are known to be on top of the game. There was excitement everywhere. Downtown was filling up with people. There were tens of thousands of people in red. Everyone was rearranging their evening to be ready for the game.

The stadium was located in the middle of downtown St. Louis in the shadow of the Arch. It was going to be a good day.

On my third call of the day, I entered the home and got a big hug from my patient's family member. She said, "Are you ready for the game?" I told her that I was more than ready and that we were going to kick the Dodgers' ass. That's how I talk sometimes if the other person has talked to me the same way in the past. I finished up with my patient, and while I was visiting with the family in the living room, watching the pep rally in downtown St. Louis, a newsflash came on the TV.

"Two people were murdered in downtown St. Louis just a few minutes ago near Busch Stadium," the announcer said. We all looked at each other. There goes the little bit of the happiness we all had. Their mother is dying, there was extreme tension in the streets from the Ferguson situation, and now some idiots had just killed two people almost in the middle of the St. Louis Cardinals pep rally.

Now I know what people mean when they say, "The life is sucked out of your face." The life was sucked out of our faces. We were all pissed off and mostly sad that we had been brought back to the reality of the violence that surrounded us.

One family member commented, "Can't they knock off that shit for one goddamn day." The others nodded in agreement. At that moment, I think we all felt the same. I didn't say anything. I shook my head a little and got my much-needed "goodbye hug" and left.

There had been a car chase, I later found out, that ended in downtown St. Louis. Shots were fired from one car into another. The car from which the shots were fired held five people, two of whom were killed. A variety of drugs were found in the car in packets that appeared to be intended for street sale.

Two people died that day. I couldn't help but wonder who really cared about these murder victims. I cared. Their families certainly cared. The baseball game was played, of course. There was no moment of silence at the game for those who had died. All I could think was, *what a whole bunch of horribleness*! After a couple more calls, I went home exhausted and went to bed early knowing I would miss the game. What wears me out is that it appears there is nothing on the horizon that indicates things will ever get better.

After I leave work, I always go home to a fairly safe neighborhood. I choose to work where these people live. They have no choice. That also makes me sad.

"For some patients, happiness is certain pain medications. For others, it's a McDonald's cheeseburger."
—Tia Rees

CHAPTER 17

They Can Kiss My Black Ass

By October, the federal prosecutors released—or perhaps it would be more accurate to say—leaked information about the Michael Brown shooting. It indicated that there had been a scuffle in the police car, that two shots had been fired inside the vehicle, that Brown's blood had been on the gun, inside the car and on the officer's clothing, suggesting that Mike Brown had been shot while his hand or arm had been in the police car.

The whole city was abuzz. *What did this mean? Why did they release this information?* After all, the grand jury was supposedly a secret endeavor and had not yet completed its work. The new information was used by those on the officer's side to bolster their position that the police officer had just been doing his job. The defenders of Mike Brown said that the newly released information did not change their minds about Mike Brown being gunned down in the street when he was probably trying to surrender. Some also thought that the federal government released the details to begin to prepare those who supported Mike Brown's innocence for the possibility that there would not be charges against the officer.

In any case, the protests continued around the city, and everyone was talking about the wild times we would all experience if the grand jury decided there would be no indictment.

Al Sharpton announced that he would be coming back to Ferguson soon for four days, each day representing the four hours Mike Brown's body had lain in the streets. This was an important issue for the supporters of Mike Brown. I think that both sides recognized that leaving his body in the street for so long was unacceptable.

As the days wore on, some were taking in the information and molding it into their own view of the events—ending with where there their thought process had been at the beginning.

The grand jury announcement was about four weeks away.

Some might expect that I might have been a little nervous to visit my patients under these circumstances, but it made no difference to me. I knew they would tell me what they thought and some really wanted to know what this little white girl was thinking. I am always extremely careful about what I say, but what I have learned is to try to listen at least twice as much as I talk. God gave us two ears and one mouth for this reason.

Taking care of the patient is always my main focus. Taking care of the patient's family is the next focus. As part of both, I always try to have conversations that cheer them up or at least reassure them. I have learned that after we cover the medical issues, the conversation usually moves to baseball, sports in general, and current events. I'm lucky I can talk some football with the best, I know enough about baseball (including that Mike Matheny, the Cardinals' manager, is so handsome that he could never make a mistake), and I am well informed about politics and current events.

I used to say about my opinion that, "My favorite color is plaid." That won't work, however, when trying to gain someone's trust. They want to know what you think, and anything else is an insult to them and they won't befriend you. What's important is how you present your thoughts and opinions. Sometimes, in fact, many times, I do not give my opinion while on the job because it may create a problem in my relationship with the patient or the family.

In these cases, I try to turn the conversation back to them or just tell them that I am still formulating my views. Sometimes after I do this, they start guessing what I am thinking. This works for me. If they hit on an option that I know they are comfortable with, I tell them that that is where I am currently leaning. At other times, if I know that I just totally disagree with them on an issue and they push me, I just don't play my cards. I was once told that, "The less said, the less said wrong."

What comforts me is that I very seldom disagree with them.

It was actually a beautiful day, seventy degrees and sunny. I was in a good mood as I smelled the fall leaves. They were changing color to orange, yellow and red as they fell into the yards and streets. It's interesting that people love to look at the fall leaves—basically, they are dying and turning colors as they do so.

As I drove through the city, the autumn leaves and nice weather somehow made all the condemned houses, trash in the streets and foot-tall weeds look not so bad. Best of all, I had my windows rolled down and Kid Rock blasting on the radio. One of the nice things about working in these neighborhoods is that you can blast your music until you shake the windows in the houses, and folks are used to it. Of course, John was behind me in the Tahoe. As I took in the crisp fresh air, we headed to one of my patient's homes in one of the roughest areas of the city.

The home was tidy and had a clean, well-kept yard with a chain-link fence around it. Two condemned houses sat across the street, and next door to them was a vacant lot full of weeds. While this part of the block was okay, just around the corner where I have another patient, the house was in very poor condition. There were homeless people on the corner standing around and drinking their 40s while the stray dogs mingled in between them.

My patient's daughter, Jolene, had an awesome personality. She was in her early sixties and stood about five-feet two. Her wavy gray hair framed a beautiful face and a lovely smile. Jolene was meticulous in keeping the home clean, and she took excellent care of her father. She opened the door and greeted me with a smile and a hug as she led me to the kitchen.

The patient, Jolene's father, had a condition such that he really shouldn't eat. He did crave and was given a few bites of a McDonald's cheeseburger a couple of days earlier. He had a feeding tube in his stomach and was continuing this until he decided he wanted it to stop. He also had an oxygen mask on. He was alert and still of sound mind, but he could no longer get out of bed.

As I walked into the house, I could smell the cooking. Oh, the cooking! It smelled like the real food being cooked in my home when I was growing up—the kind of smell that makes you hungry. It's the kind of cooking that will immediately make you forget your diet.

Jolene's sister was at the stove cooking a roast. She invited me to eat with them and told me I should get a plate. I have to admit that if I hadn't been so busy, I would have done it. I love a home-cooked meal.

So we sat down at the kitchen table to catch up on my patient's care. Jolene had a big Bible in front of her with a highlighter next to it. She told me that she had been reading the Bible and that she felt really blessed because her father had actually eaten that day. I went into his room and assessed him from head to toe, and we discussed his needs in detail, then we returned to the table.

Jolene looked at the Bible and then looked at me. "How do you do what you do?" she asked.

I have been asked this question many times. She was referring to my working every day with persons who are dying and with their families.

I looked at Jolene and simply said, "I love doing what I do. Of course, we are all going to die and it makes me feel good that I can help patients and their families get through a difficult time. Just look at your dad and see that we as a team are making him as happy and comfortable as we can. For some patients, this means certain pain medications. For others, happiness is a McDonald's cheeseburger."

She thought about this as I went on to tell her that families like hers made what I do worthwhile. Then she clarified the real reason she had asked, but I think I had understood it as soon as she began to talk. She was thinking, *hey you are young and white and don't have to come into our neighborhood.* That is what she was thinking.

She said, "Yes, but you are in one of the worst areas of the city, and you are taking your life into your hands coming into these neighborhoods."

I looked at her again. "Everyone deserves care—no matter where they live."

She then started to talk about the rioting and how bad it had been getting. Her family owned a local business. "I walk my customers to their cars just to keep them safe," she said. "Of course, I know you bring security along with you, but I'm going to protect you, too."

With that, Jolene pulled up her sweatshirt, grabbed a gun out of her waistband, and placed a .357 pistol dead-center on the Bible. This did not surprise me—it was the reality of the times we live in. We then talked about the tone of the city and how dramatically the crimes had been increasing since the riots had begun.

Most important, we talked about there being little hope that things would ever get better. Then I received one of the best compliments I have ever gotten.

"When you walked into our home the first time, you changed the tone for the better. And somehow since you've been coming, it has been so much better. Your personality bleeds positive and you made my family feel comfortable with the situation we are in," Jolene said. "You deal with death and dying every day, but you still are comforting and in a good mood. You keep it real. Tia you have a big personality, it's a gift and you are a blessing for us."

Even though this made me feel really good, I know that all hospice nurses do the same thing. It isn't just me, it is what all of us do and is our company's mission.

Each time I went to Jolene's house we talked about race relations. This was her idea. I listened a lot, but offered my thoughts when she asked. If I ever thought something I was going to say would create a problem, I would find a way not to say it. But that just never happened with her.

So we talked. She said, "It wasn't good before this situation in Ferguson, and these young punks rioting make it worse." Then came the bomb. "Jesse Jackson and Al Sharpton can kiss my black ass!" Jolene exclaimed. All they want is their fifteen minutes on TV. They come in the city while the cameras are rolling, get the people all pumped up and then leave!"

Then she started talking about the upcoming grand jury announcement. She indicated that the outcome would most likely be in favor of the officer. Then she said, "Why can't they make the announcement in the middle of the winter? Those niggers won't come out and cause all that trouble if it is too cold." I didn't say anything.

She thought a little and then said, "Tia, it makes me so angry that you are taking care of people who can't help themselves and some don't even have family, and you have to bring security with you so those thugs don't hurt you or break into your car while you are seeing your patients."

I considered this. It was a complex issue and I wasn't sure how to respond. So I came up with, "It is what it is." That certainly wasn't the most profound statement, but it was the best I had.

On the way to my next patient visit, I thought about how cool it was that—while Jolene was taking care of her dying father and living in an unsafe area—she was angry because of what I had to go through just to take care of them. I felt that she truly cared about me, and it was a very good feeling.

CHAPTER 18

Buddy and Drug Business—but Not on My Watch

The St. Louis Post-Dispatch, the local daily newspaper, released the secret autopsy and toxicology report in October 2014. It indicated the same information the federal report contained, stating that Mike Brown was shot in the hand in the police vehicle at close range. The toxicology report also indicated that he had marijuana in his blood.

This local report seemed to be more of a reality check for everyone, perhaps because it was in the local paper. People started buzzing again, and some folks just seemed to find what they needed to support their already made-up minds.

Buddy was dying, as are all of my patients. But like a few of my patients, he was able to get in a car and "keep on keeping on." He also told me he struggled with a drug addiction. His primary doctor called me to give me a heads-up on the patient's medication usage while under our care. The doctor advised me to give him only a one-week refill of his narcotics because he was going through them in three days, which is not acceptable. But Buddy could be creative in getting his drugs. He'd even called the doctor after hours and said that he'd had a leak in his roof and his narcotics had been swept away. He needed a refill immediately, he told the doctor. Buddy had been given a thirty-day supply just three days before.

When I have new patients, I see them two days a week at a minimum once they are brought into our service. In Buddy's case, when I scheduled a visit, it was often difficult to find him. He usually wasn't there and I would have to track him down. This happened with some of my patients from time to time.

My patients cannot escape me. I hunt them down and take care of business.

After I got off work, I got a call from our answering service. They told me that Buddy had called in and wanted a refill of his medicine. Of course, they didn't refill the prescription, and they told him that he needed to see me before that could happen.

Now he was ready to talk. I called him, he answered his phone, and we set up a time and day to meet. It was high noon, and I was ready for the fight. My concern was that the medicine was disappearing. I would never accuse a patient of this, but I have to deal with reality in order to look out for the patient's health. I also must protect my nursing license and that of the physician.

John and I headed out for the visit. I was taking John for two reasons: The neighborhood was rough, and the patient had told us that there were drug deals going on regularly on his block. When we arrived, John and I came up with a plan. He would go into the house with me and if asked, tell them he was there to keep an eye on my work. He pulled a notebook and pen out of his car trunk.

We went to the door and Buddy answered, asking me who the guy with me was. I told him that sometimes they send people with me to check things out. Buddy seemed a little thrown off by this. In fact, he became very pleasant then and told us to come on in and have a seat on the couch.

We talked in detail about his illness and the issues he was dealing with. I did a complete evaluation on Buddy in the other room, while he was still freaking out about John's presence. John was sitting on the couch taking notes or writing down a grocery list or something.

Once the assessment was complete, I told him I knew he had called the service last night to request a prescription refill. He grew very quiet. I moved to the floor, sitting cross-legged to have an earnest discussion with Buddy. (I have learned that you never want to be hanging over patients when you are communicating with them. I try to get on an equal or a lower level. They generally respond better this way.) In a very nice way, I told Buddy that I could absolutely refill his prescription, but that I needed to see the empty bottles and do a quick count on his meds. I explained that he would get a one-week refill at a time.

I told him that the only people who could provide him with the refills were me, the doctor or the nurse practitioner. This is where it always gets a little tough for me. I have to be nice—but firm. He had gone from being concerned to being happy that he wasn't in trouble or going to jail. He looked a little relieved, so I thought this would be a good time to speak his language and make my point in a way he might remember.

So I said with a smile, "If your roof leaks and the drugs are swept away, there will not be a refill." He took that comment so well that I added another. "If you flush them down the toilet accidentally, there will not be a refill." He actually smiled at this and then I smiled, too. We were doing some real communicating here on the floor. He knew I knew. I ended with, "There will be no refills if you drop them on the floor. Just pick them up and blow off the dirt, because God made dirt and it don't hurt."

By this point, he was kind of smiling, so I told him to get the bottles so that I could count them and call in a refill. He got up and went to the bedroom and came out with the bottles of medicine. I put the bottles on the coffee table and opened each one, counting the medications out loud as John appeared to write them down.

I made sure not to look over at John because I was afraid that I might laugh. I was just thinking how great it was to have him there, willingly play-acting his role. He didn't have to do it. This definitely wasn't part of his job description. I think he did enjoy it, however, and he knew he was helping me and the patient. John likes helping people.

So I went through the bottles, finally getting to the main medication. There were only three pills left. Buddy was also on another drug for pain, which I think was the medication that was truly working best for him.

The primary medications were accounted for, so I reminded Buddy that he would not get any refills until next week. He nodded his head and said okay.

I looked him in the eye and could tell that, just like a six-year-old, he was going to test us again.

"I know that you are going to wait a few days and test the answering service and call in for refills," I said.

He looked at me very seriously and said, "Miss Tia, I won't ever do that."

I looked him right back in the eye and said, "Yes, you will. You are going to test the system, but I can assure you that there will not be any refills called in except by me, the doctor, or the nurse practitioners."

Things were calm in the home. I reviewed all of the issues he was dealing with and made sure that we were addressing all of them. I smiled just to remind him that I cared about him and his illness.

Two nights later I was at home watching TV on the couch, my two kitty cats beside me. The answering service called to let me know that Buddy—my Buddy—had just called and placed a "super-sized" order of drugs.

I smiled and petted the cats and continued calmly watching my TV show.

Tia 1, Buddy 0. He didn't get the drugs. I liked Buddy. I thought that perhaps I was just like the grade school teacher who takes a liking to the troubled student. There is just a little something special about them—even if they make mischief.

CHAPTER 19

The Coffin in the White People's Front Yard

The news one evening in late October said that there were four murders in St. Louis the night before. Three of these were in the general area I served. The protesting had picked up. The police had needed to draw their weapons as the rioters were throwing bottles of water at them. Of course, our area made the national news again because of all the protests. I found myself wondering how these individuals found the time to protest as often as they do. The news coverage included parents bringing their youngsters to the protests just so that they could be part of history. *What historical event were they thinking this would be?* If there is true change, I thought, it will be remembered. That is what I was hoping for.

That day had also been a national day of protest across the nation to end police brutality, so the news channel showed events in other major cities around the country.

It was reported that the St. Louis crime rate thus far in 2014 had just reached the entire total of the previous year's number. I couldn't help but think that things were about to get worse. It was mid-October and we not only had a long way to go, but the "big announcement" was yet to come.

Today my first visit was to a white couple who lived in my territory. Yes, there are white families mixed in with the African Americans. There aren't many of them, but more than I had ever thought. Most of them live there because their family planted roots there many years ago. They stay because they are either content there or really can't afford to move. There are also more and more mixed-race couples living there.

With John behind me, we set out for their home. As we rolled up to the home, I caught a glimpse of something big in the front yard. I am used to seeing things in front yards. People in the areas I serve tend to use the whole yard. They don't waste the front for just a lawn. As I stopped my vehicle, it was clear that the large object on the lawn was a coffin. *Okay, so it's close to Halloween,* I thought. Maybe it was the beginning of a nice display for the neighborhood children. The coffin was big and silver. As I got out of my car, another thought popped into my head.

Maybe my patient is getting it ready for his trip to heaven. John got out of his vehicle and gave me a look that said, "What the hell is that thing doing in the front yard?" His vehicle was close to mine and he saw me simply shrug my shoulders.

As I walked to the front door, Ron was coming out. He still was getting around fairly well. "Hey Tia, how the hell are you?" he said.

I was still gaping at the coffin. I noticed some colorful stickers on it that had to do with car racing. I didn't say hi. "What the hell is a coffin doing in your front yard?" I said.

About that time, his wife Becky came out the front door and said, "Hey, Tia."

"What is that thing doing in your front yard, Becky?" I asked again.

Ron jumped in and said he was making a toolbox out of it. He grabbed me by the arm like a father showing someone their new firstborn in the crib and began describing how it was set up. He showed me all the compartments he had built to the perfect size and specifications for each of his tools.

John was in his vehicle and I wondered what he was thinking. For all he knew, the coffin held a dead dog. I turned to John and gave him the thumbs up. I didn't go over and explain because I wanted him to wonder about the coffin for just a little longer.

When this had been cleared up, we went into the home and got down to medical business. We sat in the living room and he said he wanted to go over a few things. Ron took great care of himself and always followed the program. He told me that he was getting ready for a four-day deer hunt down in the rural part of Missouri. I told him I know all about that, as my family members were hunters. I told him that he and Becky should do as many of the things they could do and wanted to do. Hospice supports that, I told them. We encourage our patients to live until they die.

He told me that he had just wanted to make sure it was cool because he did not want to lose me as his nurse. "Tia, you do a great job taking care of us, he said. "I don't want to screw it up." Then he said that he wanted to go to Nashville. He seemed a little nervous telling me this.

I explained to him and Becky that, because of the time it would take and the treatment he needed, he would most likely have to drop our service and then re-up when he returned. I had to start thinking about what we could do to make this happen for the dying man.

"Well, then, we will cancel the Nashville trip, because we ain't losing you as our nurse," Ron declared.

I gave it some thought and finally said, "Ron, here's what we might be able to do. We'll call Nashville and hook you up with a hospice program there during your visit, and then we'll re-hook you back up with us when you return."

Ron offered the idea of just not telling anyone. He would fly under the radar, he said—just go and take his medication with him.

I stood up to make a point and think better. I hesitated and then calmed down and said, "Ron, *you* are the patient, and we need to find a way to accomplish what you want."

"Just forget the Nashville trip," he said, shaking his head. "We don't want to lose you as our nurse."

At this point, I had a plan. "Let me get on the phone and see what I can do," I said to Ron. After calling our social worker and a few other people while out on the porch, I went back in the living room and gave them good news.

"We are good to go," I told them. "You can do the deer hunt and the trip to Nashville. We have a hospice contact in Nashville who will take care of you while you are there."

They were so happy. They said that this was why they never wanted to lose me: I make things happen. We hugged, and I went out and told John there was no dead body in the coffin. We laughed together.

This is what hospice people do. This is also what my co-workers do. We make things happen. We try to work on anything that improves the final days for the patient and family. We want them to *really live* until they die.

Note: The cover photo is the actual coffin/tool box I refer to in this chapter.

CHAPTER 20

They Are Just Babies, for God's Sake-SHOT!

It was a beautiful, warm Saturday in October. While normally I work Monday through Friday from eight to four-thirty, sometimes I work Saturdays. Sometimes I work Saturday and Sunday. Sometimes I'm on call for twenty-four hours. Sometimes it seems I work all the time.

Saturdays can be laid back. Maybe I dress a little more casually or even eat a donut—a change from the healthy diet I follow during the week. On Saturdays the patients and their families are more relaxed and in a better mood.

Just because it was Saturday did not mean I didn't need to feed my addiction at Starbucks. I drove up as usual, and many of the same cars were on the lot. I headed to the counter and they already knew what I would order. On the counter sat a regular coffee and a green tea. I sat down as usual and opened up my computer. While waiting for the laptop to boot up, I looked around.

All of the regulars were all dressed down—t-shirts, baseball hats, sweat pants and sneakers on them all. They also seemed more relaxed and took just a little more time with each of their greetings, so I smiled across the shop a few times and the world was all good. I checked my schedule and took a few sips of my drug of choice and headed out the door.

Even though we were well into October, it was totally a summer day. I would have put my top down, but I don't have a convertible. I set off on my regular route to see my first patient. He had not been doing well and had a really rough night. I got to his home and went inside, sitting down with him and the family members. He said, "Tia, I am so glad to see you." We talked and made some necessary adjustments to his treatment plan, and then he told me all he wanted to do was sleep.

He thanked me again for coming and I went into the other room to give the family an update. He had a wife and four children who took great care of him. We went over the new plan and I made sure they had no questions. The mother gave me a hug, and I was off to the next visit.

I got into Lola, took a couple gulps of green tea, and set out for my next home. As I was turning down a regular street I often took on my route, I saw at least fifteen police cars, half with their lights still on. They were all in the streets surrounding a church. Police were everywhere. Then I saw that yellow "crime scene" tape all around the church and the parking lot. Traffic was jammed and the police cars were parked sideways. I had to pull over and park because traffic could not pass.

What in the world was going on? I wondered. It was a beautiful day, we were at a church, and I was sick of violence. In fact, the whole city was sick of violence.

I got out of the car. In front of where I parked, a full-scale barbecue fundraiser was going on. There were seven middle-aged women cooking, getting plates ready and taking money. I thought that maybe whatever was happening could be good news. They weren't worried about the police and the yellow tape. Business was good, and they were thanking everyone for their support and chatting as if they were on a neighbor's front porch.

I felt a little relief. I walked around the barbecue stand and saw a small crowd in the church parking lot. They were mostly police officers, but there were also several people standing around crying and hugging one another.

There are different kinds of crying. I cry quietly to myself and try to hold back as much as I can. Most men cry as little as possible. As I got a clear shot of the people standing there, I saw that they were crying for real. *This is bad,* I thought.

I didn't get close, but I could see a police officer I knew over on the edge of the parking lot. He's a great guy that I have talked to a few times, and he always waves to me when I see him. He always shakes his head each time I see him to remind me that he thinks I am crazy for working in the area.

I went over to him and he turned around. I could see he had been crying, too. I started to tear up myself. "What's wrong? What happened?" I asked him.

He quickly pulled himself together. "A little two-year-old girl was just shot in a drive-by," he said. "I think she's going to be okay, though."

I was saddened to hear that a toddler had been shot, but relieved that she would be okay. I was also pissed off at the shooters.

"There were people outside, but nobody saw anything," he said.

What? I thought. *Come on, people, take a risk and get child killers off the streets.*

The church was very close to where some of my patients lived. I was concerned that possibly this little girl might be the child or grandchild of one of my patients. I asked for a name, but he didn't have one. He told me they took her to Children's Hospital.

Neither of us wanted to say much, so we just looked at one another and said to be safe. Police and hospice nurses are buds. Police officers look out for us as their time permits. Many of them have followed me to ensure my safety. We share information as it relates to safety issues. I have a great deal of respect for what police do. I'm sure there are some who aren't perfect, but I have been fortunate not to meet many of them.

I walked away feeling angry that the little girl had been shot for no reason. As I was walking by the barbecue booth, I couldn't help but wonder what in the world was going through the minds of those seven women working there just after the poor child had been shot.

I wasn't hungry and only eat barbecue on special occasions, but something— I think it was just curiosity—made me walk right up to the booth. I told myself to order a plate. After all, the money was going to a good cause in the community. I placed my order and looked for something in the lady's eyes to give me an answer. Her eyes told me that she was just a lady selling barbecue.

Surely she and the women in the booth have children and maybe grandchildren, I thought. I looked around at the other ladies. There was no indication from any of them that they were selling barbecue in the middle of a war zone. I moved down the line to pick up my plate. The lady in the booth had her back to me, but then turned around with the plate. Our eyes met. Her eyes held not just the sadness for that one little child being shot, but also for all the others who had been similar innocent victims.

I could tell she saw the same thing in my own eyes. She was black and I was white, but that didn't enter into this. People are people and children are children and a two-year-old is still a baby. She handed me my plate and I said, "God bless you and be safe." She could see that I was very upset. She grabbed my arm and said, "You too, child."

I walked across the street and got into Lola and cried. How can this happen? A child is playing in front of a Church and some thugs drive by and shoot her. I will never understand how people live in communities where this type of thing happens on a regular basis. What is worse is that there don't seem to be any real solutions on the horizon.

I finished the rest of my calls, which made me feel a little better, and took Lola home. I smelled the barbecue in my back seat all the way home and was beginning to get a little hungry. I rolled up to my house, got the barbecue out and went in the house. I petted my beautiful kitties and sat on the couch, popping on the TV.

As I busted open the plate of food, it was time for the evening news. I used to think that the news was just about the world, the city, some weather, and of course, the best part for me, the sports. Now I watch it to find out what is going on near and around my place of work.

The leadoff story was about the little two-year-old girl. Her father was interviewed and he explained that he had been standing right next to his daughter when multiple gunshots struck her legs. I was thinking about when my brother once had told me that a lot of the poor people who own guns find that the guns don't work when they use them. Many folks don't know how to shoot them properly, and often they load the wrong bullets in them. He also explained that many gangs may require a member to shoot someone in order to increase their status in the gang. Shooting out of a moving car makes the shots even less accurate, so they miss a lot and quite often hit the wrong targets.

The father said that after his toddler had been shot, he had just held her and screamed, "Why?" He went on to say that she cried for five minutes as he held her. Soon, however, she had looked up at him and said, "Daddy, I am okay."

He said he got strength from his little girl to cope with the tragedy.

The next story on the news was about another drive-by in North St. Louis on one of the blocks where I have a patient. A four-year-old was shot in the ankle while sitting on a porch. As the report continued, they said there were no witnesses. No witnesses—again. We all know there are no witnesses because the residents of these neighborhoods are afraid of retaliation. That always pisses me off. I know I don't live there and can't imagine what it is really like, but I would think that if someone shot a little child, anyone who saw anything would turn them in. How could you live with yourself if you didn't? Maybe someday I will understand this, but not on this day. I was just angry.

CHAPTER 21

Stag Beer, Vanilla Ice Cream and Death

It was mid-November, and the whole community awaited the ruling from the grand jury. Some thought it would come after the election—which was just around the corner. The official indication was that the ruling would take a few more weeks. The Justice Department had leaked that they may not have enough evidence for a civil rights case against the Ferguson Police Department. Eric Holder declared that the Ferguson Police Department needed wholesale changes. Some believed that information was being leaked because the grand jury would not be handing down a decision to have a trial. Others like me were just waiting for the announcement.

A sense of impending doom gripped the area. Many people were stocking up on essentials at their homes because there was a real concern that "all hell could break loose" if the decision was that there would not be a trial. The schools requested that there be a one-day advance warning before the decision so that they could make sure the children got home safely. Community leaders, political figures and other heavyweights spent four days in Ferguson to ask people to stay calm no matter the outcome of the grand jury.

So we waited. I carried supplies for myself and my kitties in my trunk and made reservations at my parents' house just across the river. While I lived a good distance from my territory, there had been a spate of recent shootings not that far away from where I live. I also stocked up my patients with their drugs and other supplies just in case I could not visit them or their medications could not be delivered.

As I was driving to visit a patient one day, I thought about how tough it must be for the families. They were dealing with the death of a loved one and then they had to contend with all of this other drama. It seemed unfair.

I will say that most of the folks I served were tough enough to cope with both types of crises at once, maybe because they were used to danger. We talked about it openly every day. They would show me their stockpiles and their weapons and tell me that they were ready to take care of "those fools," as they called them. They also reassured me that they would keep me safe.

I arrived at the home of one of my favorite families. This was Vera's home, and she was taking care of her dying husband. Vera was a terrific, caring person. I parked Lola, and as I got out, I always looked around and then moved into the house quickly. Vera greeted me with a smile and said that she was happy to see me. When people are taking care of someone who is dying, they love to have company, and our job in hospice is to take care of them, too. Sometimes my patients' family members seem surprised when we show concern for them, but we are responsible for the entire family.

Vera's smile faded and what remained was the normal concern and worry she always had on her face. We talked a little, and then I did a complete assessment of her husband. I went into the living room and we discussed the current and upcoming care program for her husband.

When business was over, I asked her how she was doing. She said that she was fine but had lots of thoughts going through her mind. I could see in her eyes exactly what she meant. I have seen it many times before. I knew I needed to draw her out to leave her feeling okay about what she was thinking.

One of the problems in the world is that people say one thing but often mean something very different. The best communicators are able to say what they think and also get the other person to do the same. That was my mission.

There comes a point in many dying situations when an individual may be ready for their loved one to die, but they hide this and don't think it appropriate to verbalize it. They think that feeling this way is uncaring. My job is not to tell them how to think or feel but to convince them that they are not the first to have these feelings, and that maybe that is okay.

Vera's husband's condition was extremely bleak, and he was not really responsive anymore.

"Vera, have you been wondering why your husband has been lingering so long?" I gently inquired.

She seemed reluctant to comment, but finally spoke. "As the days have gone by, I have been having some thoughts about that," she acknowledged.

"Is it possible you feel a little guilty for having thoughts like that?" I asked. She started to cry at this.

"All of this is normal and okay," I assured her. Then she really cried. "Your motives are very good and I know you don't want your husband to continue to suffer. I know that this is not an issue of you being unwilling to take care of him."

The crinkles of concern left her face. "How do people hang on for so long when the body seems to be finished?" she asked.

I had to do some quick thinking. I will never tell people that we should want somebody to die, but I am in the business of keeping people alive and as comfortable as possible *while* they die. So what the hell could I say? I settled on telling her what others have told me.

I told Vera that I have had other families in exactly the same situation and that they, too, had the same feelings. The difference was that they said what they were thinking and they said it to me. I have heard it many times. I have had family members tell me that they wish the patient would just die so they would no longer be in pain. They just couldn't stand to watch their loved one suffer.

At other times, the family would even joke about it and say, for example, that their dad was staying alive just to piss them off because that was the type of person he was. I have also been in a situation where there was a whole house full of family members dividing up all the household contents while the patient was still dying in the other room. For some reason this did not bother me because they had taken superior care of their father and they were a great family. They had been sitting around for weeks and finally someone spoke up and started going through old pictures and other items, and then the process blossomed into "who gets what." There was a whole lot of, "Oh no, you take that," and, "Dad would have wanted you to have that." A great deal of nervous energy was released. They even offered me a couple of items that were sports related, but I didn't accept them because I realized they were just trying to include me in the process.

This process seemed normal and healthy to me. The family's father had been unresponsive for some time, and they had accepted that he was going to die. In a way, they were moving on with their lives.

By this time, I think Vera was starting to feel a little better. She asked me what keeps these patients alive when the medical people say that they should be dead. I told her that I wasn't sure but I could tell her what other families have told me. I told Vera that one family member told me that sometimes when the body is done, the soul still may have unfinished business on the earth. This family member had gone on to tell me that the loved one will hang on until the business is complete.

I told Vera that I have seen many cases of this. For example, some patients have told me they were waiting for a son who was in prison to come see them. Other patients have told me they were waiting for a son or daughter to come home from the military. I told Vera that I have made many arrangements for these loved ones to get home in time. Still other patients have told me they were waiting for Christmas.

Vera was opening up. "What is my husband waiting for, Miss Tia?" she asked.

I told her that I really didn't know. I was a little nervous, so I kept on talking. I told Vera that sometimes families have told me they were waiting for that special grandson or granddaughter to visit them. I told her about a recent situation where a young boy was afraid to come to the house to see his dying great-grandfather. I talked to the family and arranged for a counselor to meet with the boy at the home. The grandson visited his grandpa and then the grandpa passed away that very evening.

I could see that Vera liked hearing these stories, but they weren't necessarily answering her question. She had no idea what her husband was waiting for. So I took a different approach. I told Vera that perhaps we didn't know what he was waiting for, but based on what she had told me about her relationship with him, that I thought he would want her to start living again as best she could under the circumstances.

I told Vera that sometimes families believe they need to tell the dying family member that it is okay if they go. I went on to tell her that some people think that the dying person is hanging on for them, and that if they just tell them that, the patient will die in peace. I also told her that I have witnessed this many times. Even in cases where the patient is unresponsive, when this is done, the patient often passes soon after.

She looked at me, and I knew I was finally onto something. I told Vera that I knew she had a full life with lots of friends and that she was very active in the church. She nodded in agreement. I looked her in the eye and told her that she needed to make some changes and get out of the house more. Furthermore, I said, that is exactly what her husband would most likely want. I said all of this in a very matter-of-fact way.

Vera looked at me as if I was the mom and she was the daughter. She admitted that she did miss getting out and seeing all her friends. I told her that, as of that moment, that would be changing. I also told her that I knew that she had some family members who had been offering to help watch her husband and that we would call them immediately to get her some free time to get out of the house.

I told her that she needed to give herself permission to not be there all the time—even that unknown time when he would pass away. I told her that would be okay. She had done enough.

Vera asked me if I really thought that this was okay, and I assured her that I was certain it was okay.

Vera was getting excited. I told her that we needed to turn on a few more lights around the house and open up the curtains and the windows. She agreed and said, "The place looks like someone is dying here." We both laughed.

Vera had a new lease on life—*her* life. She said that she would only want to go to church and do a little shopping, but she might want to start cooking a little more. I told her that I knew that she liked to have the occasional cigarette and a little brandy once in a while, and that she should bring it out. She said that once she brightened up the place, maybe people would stay longer when they visited.

Vera told me that when her husband had grown seriously ill, she had more or less shut the house down and refrained from smoking and drinking. She asked me if I really thought it would be okay to liven up the place. I told her that she had to do this, and that this was exactly what her husband would want. She said, "Well then, okay, Miss Tia, if that is what you think."

Jesus, I was thinking. *What have I done?* Then, *Who cares? She is happy.* I hoped that all I had done was simply to give her permission for what she really had been wanting to do anyway. It's human nature to seek external confirmation or permission for something our hearts have already been telling us.

"I'm just not real sure about the smoking," Vera said. "What do you think?"

As she went into the kitchen to get us a couple of cans of Coke, an image of a real party breaking out came into my mind. I told Vera that I have been in homes full of cigarette smoke and the smell of a bar. These were the homes of good people one and all, just dealing with the situation. "If you don't allow smoking and drinking," I said, "then smokers and drinkers won't come to see you and they won't stay if they come."

I went on to say that I have been in a home where there was weed on the kitchen table. Vera handed me my Coke and said, "God, Miss Tia, you see it all, don't you?" Then I said that she might want to add a little music. I'm not sure why I said that; it just came to me, but it actually was not a bad idea.

She took a belt of the ice-cold Coke long enough that her eyes watered a little, but I noted that this wasn't tears. I was thinking she was good to go. She asked if I could stay for just a few more minutes to finish the soda and I told her I certainly could.

It was clear that the stories—and permission to live her life—were helping her to feel better, so I asked her if I could tell her about some of my patients and what they were up to during their last days. She said to go ahead.

I told her about the fear some families have in granting the last wishes of dying family members on simple things. I described the day I walked into a home and the family was arguing about their dad wanting to drink and eat ice cream. As soon as I got into the living room, one of the daughters walked up to me and said that her father wanted to drink Stag beer and eat vanilla ice cream—and that she was sure that he should not do that.

I had responded, "For God's sake, if he wants Stag and ice cream, let him have it!" Half the room cheered and the other half was mad at me. The outcome was that every day he drank beer and ate ice cream. I told Vera that I tried to make the patient as comfortable as possible and that I always monitored the patient very carefully to make sure the beer and ice cream didn't harm him. I went through other stories of people who wanted McDonald's food, and the family felt they had to get my permission. Other patients have wanted ice cream shakes and I was always happy to buy them and bring them to their homes.

Vera then said that she was surprised that some families are comfortable drinking and smoking in the same house as a dying loved one. I told Vera that I'd just had a situation like that.

Just a few days before, I had gone to a home where there were four daughters taking care of their dying father, I told her. I walked in and did my business with the patient, and one of the girls asked me if we could talk things over. I replied that I'd wanted to review everything with them anyway, so we covered the care of their father. They seemed comfortable with me. One of the girls even said, "Hey, you are pretty cool and seem like someone we can really talk to."

"Let it rip," I told the girl, and they all laughed. The one daughter who seemed to be the oldest told me what had happened when they first hired our service. She said that when they had just brought their father home from the hospital, they were all sitting around talking about him and the fact that he was dying. They cried, then talked about what a great father he had been, and then cried some more. She went on to say that one of the girls said she needed a drink, so she went to the well-stocked cabinet and brought out a bottle of wine. She told me that an hour later, each one of them had drunk at least a bottle each while they talked about their father.

They all looked at me to see if they had my approval. I smiled mysteriously and waited just long enough to make them wonder. Then I said, "You all are just a bunch of bad people!" and laughed. I told them that it sounded like they were starting the grieving process with a little help from the wine.

"That's not the best part," one of the other daughters said. "We forgot that the hospice service would be sending you. We were all totally drunk and cleaned up in a hurry. We were really afraid. We hid all of the wine bottles and started chugging coffee. Then the doorbell rings and it's your bright face standing there."

She said that by then she believed they were more or less sober and they got through the nursing visit process somehow. Well, at least they thought they appeared sober, but a nurse is in the business of picking up on that.

We had all laughed, and I reassured them that everyone deals with these situations differently. They then told me again how cool I was, which I always like to hear, of course.

Vera was laughing by now, too. "You always have the best stories," she said.

I instructed Vera to get on the phone and call someone to pop by and start taking some shifts. "You need to change the mood of the house so others feel welcome," I said. We made the calls and the people on the other end wondered why they had not been asked to help earlier.

With all of this accomplished, I headed for the door. As I was leaving, Vera said, "I love you, Miss Tia, and you be safe."

I went outside feeling pretty good that day, but also exhausted. The Coke had given me a little boost. As I walked to my car, I was approached immediately by a neighbor kid. I had seen him before and we knew one another. He told me that I should get the hell out of the neighborhood because there had just been a shooting on the next block. He went on to tell me the best route out and advised me to be careful. He said, "You be safe now, Miss Tia." I thanked him and told him also to take care of himself.

CHAPTER 22

Sometimes You May Not Want a Medical Person Taking Care of You

One day I had to run all the way across the metropolitan area to the really nice part of the town, an upscale neighborhood where all the rich people live. This was a forty-minute drive, but sometimes we just don't have enough staff, and we need to cover for one another. There is a vast difference between my regular patients and their families and those in the more affluent areas. In my regular territory, my patients and families are usually just glad to see me and ready to follow my instructions. I am used to this.

When I go into the rich part of town, it is different—not bad, just different. When individuals have worked hard and accumulated a little money, they are able to spend it doing more for the dying family member. That is a good thing, and I am always glad to see the great care these patients receive. It makes my job easier. There is also greater expectation from these people. This is good for me and it keeps me sharp. It is also not a problem because I have the right appearance, the right vehicle, a great education, tons of experience and a good attitude. I am confident in myself and my abilities.

The families are very gracious and treat me quite well. They always ask me if I'm coming back, and when I tell them that most likely I will not be returning, they seem disappointed. When they find out where I usually work, they are shocked and say that they can't imagine how I do it.

So I headed out to the call that day without security and feeling safe, even though this would be my first time there. I was told that they had called in several times, once just to have someone come out and change the diapers on their mother. They also called with a variety of valid questions which would help them take great care of their mother.

I was also told that one of the daughters was in the medical field. I was glad to hear that. Medical or clinical experience can be a great help in these end-of-life situations.

When I arrived, I entered a really nice home and received an excellent reception. The daughter who worked in the medical field greeted me. One other daughter was present as well. We went into the living room and had a little visit, and I told them that I was ready to assess their mother. The daughter followed me upstairs and into one of the bedrooms.

When we got there, I conducted my assessment, but I could tell that probably the patient was not being adequately cared for. I could smell urine and see the dried sweat on her bedsheets. By this time, the other girl had come up to the room. I asked if their mother's bedding had been changed recently, and they told me that someone had come out and changed it and instructed them on how to do it. The daughter then remarked that she was glad I was there so I could show her again.

You've got to be kidding me, I thought. *You're in the medical field and can't change your own mother's bedding?*

Actually, I had seen cases like this before. This daughter was most likely a great caregiver, but now she was mixed up and not able to do for her mother what she had done so many times before for other patients. For some people, nursing their own loved one is just too difficult. People outside our profession would not understand this. For some of us, it is one thing to take care of hundreds of strangers, but it is quite another thing entirely to do the same for someone they are close to. This is okay; that's what we are there for.

I kept my cool and told the daughters that I would be glad to show them how to change the bedding. We cleared the blankets and the smell grew worse. I moved the poor woman onto her side and could not believe what was revealed. There was at least two days of dried urine stuck to her body and all over the sheets. I told the daughters that we were going to move her mother using the sheets and I instructed them to get some clean bedding and hot soapy water. They offered no help to me in moving her, and one of the girls didn't even come close. I told the daughter to get me a trash bag for the bedding so that they could wash it later. She said they would just be throwing it away.

The patient was very large, but I was so mad about this poor woman's condition that pure anger helped me lift her 200-pound body. Hell, I was so ticked off that I could have lifted her *and* the bed into the air. Without any help, I moved this big woman, cleaned her up perfectly, put on the new bedding and then turned to the daughter who was in the medical field. "And where did you work?" I couldn't help but ask. She told me where she worked, which was a relief because I had been afraid that she had picked up on what I really had meant, which was, "What kind of a person are you who could leave your own mother in this condition?"

I calmed down as the adrenaline fled my body and asked them if they now knew how to change the bedding. They told me they would be hiring someone to do that and that this person would be coming the next day. I was relieved for the mother.

The good news for me was that they had no clue what I was thinking and that help was on the way. I can't help what I think and couldn't avoid that initial rush of anger, but once I calmed down, I realized that they did care—they just couldn't do what I thought needed to be done. They were afraid to do it because this was their own mother. I could see that they were relieved, and we all began making small talk as they thanked me for showing them how to do something they would not be doing anyway.

The daughter then asked if I could order a special lotion that she had been putting on her mother's skin. She showed me the bottle, and I told her that I would see if the pharmacy had it. I called the pharmacy and learned that they had never heard of this particular product. She went on and on about how important this lotion was. She said she might have to ship some in and suggested that this was a product we should consider for all of our patients. I could see that she had several bottles, and knowing her mother would not live long, it seemed they would have plenty, but I told her to write down the name and that I would pass it on so that my organization could look into it. I have learned that whatever is important to these families, I get on it, and I did so immediately. She might even be right that it could benefit other patients.

As the visit wound down, I reviewed the plan, they thanked me, and I left. *I just drove forty miles one way to change a diaper on a dying patient for a daughter who is was in the medical field, I thought.* I smiled and told myself that I did help the patient. I was proud that, for the most part, I had kept my initial angry feelings to myself. *Not bad*, I thought.

Two days later, they called with the news that their mother had passed away. I was the only staff member available that day who could go to the home. I headed out of my neighborhood and drove back out to the rich people's area. I rolled up Lola in front of the house and was greeted at the front door by a nurse.

I was a little concerned about this nurse because I had been told that she had been varying the patient's prescription medicine and that she had also been instructed to stop doing this. She seemed cordial and asked me to wait in the living room as the family members were all up in the mother's bedroom grieving.

I told her that I would be going up there because I already knew the family and I had a service to provide. She explained to me that she had been taking great care of the mother and that she felt the family needed the time alone. She made the somewhat shocking mistake of talking openly about how she had adjusted the medicines to keep the patient more comfortable. I never adjust medicines without the doctor's permission. This is, in fact, illegal. I decided that we needed to do some nurse-to-nurse talking. *This ain't her mother who just died*, I thought. *Let's get it on.*

I asked her if she had been altering the administering of the meds and she admitted that she had. Because of her experience, she said, she knew of better methods than prescribed. At this point, I gave her *the look*. This is the same look parents give to teenagers who misbehave. I then advised her that I would be going up to the room. She said she preferred that I didn't.

She followed me up the steps, and I went into the room. The family members greeted me with a hug. I noticed there was a man in the room. The sisters introduced him to me as their brother. The nurse then told me she had pronounced the patient dead, and I replied that I would be doing that. I visited with the family for a little while and then told them I would wait downstairs.

The nurse followed me out of the room and asked if there was anything she could do to help. I told her my name was Tia and asked for her name and where she worked. She told me. I thank her for all she had done.

Soon the family came down the steps, and I answered a series of normal questions that come up at the time of a loved one's passing. Then the daughter began asking me if I had found out anything about the lotion. I told her that I had passed along the information to someone and that I would check back with her about this issue. This was true. I knew when she had initially asked me about the product that she was the type of person who would follow up.

One of the sisters was on the phone. The other sister asked her who she was calling and she said she was talking to the newspaper in order to get the obituary placed. There is always a lot of nervous energy at these times, and some people just have to stay busy. I understood that, but her sister told her that this could wait.

We talked for a little while longer, and the daughter mentioned that she would like to follow up with me because she had a few ideas on how we might improve our services. I told her to call me in a week, as we are always interested in making improvements. At these times, I always pay attention. Our company is big on taking suggestions and welcomes the opportunity to improve our services. These families absolutely know what they want and need, and the more we listen, the better we will be.

At this point, the brother came in. He had needed to go outside to think and be alone. It seemed that he was taking his mother's death very hard. He walked over to me, looking at my face. I was thinking at that moment that I would need to think fast and come up with some consoling words to help him get through this terrible day of loss.

"Hey, that is one real nice car you have," he said. *Huh, your mom just died and you're admiring my car*, I thought. Then one of his sisters chimed in and asked me what kind of car I had. I told her that it was an Audi. Her brother then told them that it was a bright, shiny red Audi. I realized that by having this car, they were able to accept me a little more readily.

When it was time to go, we all hugged, and I told them to stay in touch if they needed anything.

I went to my car and got out the phone number of the nursing service and called them. I told them that it was illegal for their nurse to be changing doctor's orders and that I felt they needed to know. They said they were happy I had called and would take care of it. I put the nurse's actions in my report in case I would be advised that I would need to take any other action. I have no other option in matters like this. When rules are broken or anything illegal takes place, we do not look the other way.

Actually, in the short time I was able to be with this family, I think that we all got along pretty well. When someone is dying, I am used to all kinds of people acting in all kinds of ways, and so the situation with the bed linens or the son's remarks about my Audi did not surprise me. These were good people who were just trying to do the best they could in taking care of their mother. We have to be understanding and realize that people's actions and what they say or do at such times may not always be on target or appropriate. This is human nature and that is why we are there.

CHAPTER 23

"F" Those People

One morning I was awakened very early by a text on my work phone. The text was from my supervisors and indicated that this might be the day when the grand jury ruling would come down on the Michael Brown case—a decision on whether or not there would be charges against the police officer who shot him. This text basically let us know that we should make sure our patients had all of their supplies in case we were unable to see them as a result of security issues. I had been preparing myself and my patients for this for a couple of weeks, but there were a few additional things I needed to take care of. They were looking for the announcement to be late in the afternoon that day, so I knew I had lots of work to do.

I went off to my first call and it was with one of my favorite guys—Joe. Even though he was dying, Joe was pretty alert and we always had spirited conversations. His daughter had come from the suburbs of Georgia to care for him. When I got to the home, she offered me a warm greeting. She welcomed me in, and I headed for the bedroom to check on Joe. As usual, Joe was in a good mood, greeting me with a smile and saying how glad he was to see me. As I checked him over, we discussed how he had been doing. When his daughter popped into the room, I mentioned to both of them that we had ordered some extra medicine and advised them that they might want to stock up on some essentials in case they had difficulty getting out when the grand jury announcement came down.

Joe's daughter said that she felt that nothing would happen and that they should be fine. I told her that I understood this and had just been offering a suggestion as a precaution. As I did so, I looked over at her dad—lying on his death bed. He was shaking his head where his daughter could not see it. When Joe's daughter left the room, I asked him what he was thinking. He told me his daughter was living in a fantasy world. He was very worried that they would not be able to get out of the house safely. I asked him if he wanted me to talk to her. "Yes, but she's stubborn," he said, again shaking his head.

I went into the other room where the daughter was sitting. We made a little small talk, and then she asked me what I really thought about the situation. I told her that I hoped that nothing happened, but almost everyone in the city was planning for more protests—and maybe even worse. I added that I had my items bought and that most of my patients were stocked up and ready, just in case.

She told me that she just found it hard to believe that something might happen. Keeping in mind that she'd come up from Georgia after the August shooting of Michael Brown and the following unrest, I went back and told her what the St. Louis area had experienced when the event broke out and reminded her that some believed that this time could be even worse. "This isn't the suburbs of Georgia," I told her. "Bad things are happening right now."

We both agreed on how incredibly sad and frustrating the situation seemed. She sat down and told me that maybe it wouldn't be such a bad idea to pick up a few things. I told her to head out and assured her that I would stay with her father.

She was off. I went into the bedroom and told Joe that the supplies were on the way. He smiled and told me that I was something. "Tia, I started picking cotton when I was seven years old down South and I did it 'till I was twenty. Then I moved to St. Louis and worked for the government. I started a family and also a business. My child doesn't really know how things are. I learned that the opportunity was there for me to take. I guess I protected her too much from all the bad stuff. That's what parents do."

I told Joe that he was a good father and he smiled. "Tia, you keep it real," he said. "I knew you would get that girl to go shopping. I remember when I first met you and I thought that you were something else. I immediate started liking you. You say it like it is and you know that those young punks could turn things real bad, real quick, even though you are too nice to say it."

We talked until we heard a knock at the front door. We knew this was the daughter and she wanted us to unlock the front door. I went into the living room and unlocked the three locks and the screen lock, and in she came with four plastic bags full of groceries. She thanked me for opening the door and then said, "Boy you were right, there were all kinds of people in the store in the middle of the day. Most of the milk and bread was gone, and there was a whole empty-shelved aisle where the bottles of water once were. It was weird."

I told her that she may not need any of what she bought, but it was good to have it just in case. She smiled in agreement.

I went in to check on her dad. "You're all stocked up and ready to go," I said. He seemed happy to hear this.

"Tia, I love you," he said. "You be safe out there."

I went in the kitchen, hugged his daughter and was on my way.

My next visit was across town with Robert, my patient, and Rebecca, his wife. I really like this family. Rebecca seemed always "stressed out to the max" every time I visited—and with good reason.

I rolled up and headed to the front door where Rebecca greeted me. She was just as freaked out as ever, but we knew each other well enough that she didn't act like everything was fine. I liked that. She told me to come on in to the circus.

She asked me to sit down on the couch to visit a little and discuss the change in the medications. We went over everything, and she said that it finally made sense to her. I asked her how it had been going, and she launched into a rant about how pissed-off she was because all of her husband's family and friends were asking if they could have his stuff.

Rebecca was a very nice-looking woman in good condition. She seemed well educated and dressed nicely. In fact, on this day she was even a bit more dressed up than usual. The house was very well decorated and exceptionally clean. Even when stressed out, she was normally well mannered, but I could see she had reached some kind of breaking point.

She went on to tell me which cousin wanted a certain gun and which cousin wanted some duck decoys. She continued for a while and then said, "Fuck those people, they all make me sick! I am tired of all of them. As far as I am concerned, they can all go to hell." When people are dying, their language often loosens up. The family members and patients are just too worn out to observe social niceties or to exercise the discipline they normally have.

Of course I agreed with her, partly because she was so mad that I feared she might just include me on her list if I didn't. I asked her what she was doing about it.

"I am going to let them take whatever they want," Rebecca said, "and then I will never speak to any of them ever again."

I thought this was actually a good plan, but I just kept listening, waiting for her to calm down.

I think she felt better after getting it all out there. Then we talked about their son, a young man named Bobby, who would often stop by, but he would never go in to visit his dying father. Apparently, Bobby had not seen his father for over a year and just couldn't face him. Rebecca said that he would be coming by that day. I told her that I would talk to him when he arrived to see if I could change his mind.

Robert, my patient, had been married before and had a child who was killed by his wife. His ex-wife went to prison. Rebecca had been married before and had a child who was killed by her husband, who then killed himself. I can't imagine the pain this couple had suffered.

I got up and went into Robert's room. There he was, and there was his buddy, Duke the dog. Duke was always in bed with Robert—I think Duke knew his master was dying. Duke always got off the bed when I came into the room. I was the only one he would leave for. I think he knew that it was a good time for him to take a break. I set about conducting all my normal visit procedures.

Robert was always great to talk to and opened up more each time I visited. On this visit, he told me how he wanted to have his ashes spread in the river down by the family trailer. He also told me that he wanted to go to heaven to see his son, the one who had been murdered.

This was all good news to me, because it hadn't been that long ago that he had said he didn't see any reason to keep going on once he found out he was dying. I heard the front door open and figured that it must be Rebecca and Robert's son, Bobby. I excused myself, telling Robert that I would be back in a few minutes.

I knew that I had to find a way to get their son into that room. I had no plan, but it *was* going to happen. I went into the living room and greeted Bobby. In the past, he had come and gone, and we have never really spoken to one another, but I whipped up some small talk on him and then announced that this day he would be going to visit his dad.

At this point, Rebecca left the room. I think she was scared. I told Bobby to sit down on the couch with me. I looked him right in the eye. "Together, we will make a plan," I told him. "If you don't go into that room today before your Dad passes away, you will regret it for the rest of your life. He needs to see you, and you need to do this now. All you have to do is walk over to the door with me, and step one foot inside, and then it's over."

His eyes grew wide. He had been looking straight into my eyes the entire time and had not said a word. I knew not to stop the progress. I grabbed his hand and pulled him with me over to the bedroom door, guiding him in with my hand and closing the door.

Rebecca peeked around the corner and said, "Did he go in there?"

"Yes, he did," I told her. "I have no idea of what the hell will happen in that room."

We waited together, just standing there. We were scared. A few minutes went by and then the phone rang. It was some other relative who wanted some of her husband's stuff. Rebecca told them to just come by and get it. After she hung up, she called him a son of a bitch.

More time went by, and we moved into the kitchen. Rebecca started to get teary eyed. She was happy and nervous at the same time. She looked at me and I thought that she was going to say something heavy. I prepared myself. Then she hesitated. I prepared myself some more. Then it came out, "Tia would you eat some fried hot dogs and drink some ice cream soda with us?"

I was relieved and said I would, of course. She explained that this meal was what her husband and son had always eaten years before when they'd had TV nights together. So the dogs were frying and the ice was ready for the cream soda and forty-five minutes had gone by.

Bobby emerged from the room at last. He looked as though he had cried for the entire forty-five minutes, but I thought he seemed tremendously relieved. He came into the kitchen and asked his mom if that smell was what he thought it was. Rebecca hugged him and told him that we were going to dine on dogs and cream soda. We all sat down together and had a little feast. We each ate two hot dogs and had several refills of the soda with the ice cream. We didn't talk about what was said in the room. Bobby went to the bathroom, and another call came in. All I heard was Rebecca saying, "Just take it next time you go to the trailer." Rebecca told me she didn't care anymore—she was just tired of all the calls.

Bobby stuck his head into the kitchen and said, "Mom, can I have Dad's truck?" By now Rebecca was just so happy that her son had visited his father that this was no problem. She told him to take it. Rebecca told me that it was just an old, run-down truck and not worth anything.

I finally got up to leave. I was worn out but somewhat wired from all the soda with ice cream. I checked on my patient. He was snoring and so was Duke.

Rebecca offered me a big hug and thanked me for encouraging her son to go into his father's room.

It seemed to me that these folks had dealt with so much more than I ever could. It didn't seem fair. I cranked out a short prayer for Rebecca as I drove away.

I made the rest of my calls that day, ensuring that all my patients were well stocked up on their medicines and supplies. The word was out in the homes I visited and on the street that this day would be the day of the announcement. As it turned out, that didn't happen.

CHAPTER 24

The Hospice Dating Scene

As we moved uneasily toward Grand Jury Decision Day, one afternoon I had a couple more calls to make. I showed up at a home and went inside. After I assessed the patient, I talked to the daughter, who served in law enforcement. We always spent a little time sharing our thoughts speculating on when the verdict was coming down and what could potentially transpire, depending on the outcome. After we compared notes, I said my goodbyes and headed out the front door with her.

A tall young man was out on the porch, leaning on one of the supporting posts. She saw him, but there was no alarm on her face, so I felt I was okay. I also knew she was packing and had told me many times not to worry—that she would always protect me. The man looked over at me and said, "Hey, do you need a black man in your life?"

Since I was feeling fairly secure with "the heat" nearby, I smiled and returned the banter. "I need a man in my life like a fish needs a bicycle," I replied.

He laughed, shaking his head, and said, "All I would do is ruin your credit anyway."

All three of us laughed as he walked away.

My law enforcement friend put her arm on my shoulder and told me she was wondering how I would handle that situation. "You did a great job!" she said.

We smiled at one another, and I left. As I was driving to my next visit, I thought about how the situation reminded me of an even weirder thing that had happened. I have dated a lot of different men in my life, but never found the right one. I'm good with that. It will happen someday or it won't. I have a full life, and I keep an open mind.

One day I was called to a home where a patient had just passed away. I knew the family pretty well. There was a daughter who took care of the dying father and a brother who came around once in a while. I had a good relationship with her, but I didn't know the brother very well. They lived in a fairly nice part of my territory and had a well-kept home.

I arrived at the home and talked with the daughter, who went over what had transpired with her father. I told her how sorry I was that he had passed away and that she had done one of the best jobs in taking care of him that I had ever seen.

I went into the room to do what we do when a patient passes. While doing my work, the brother came in. I figured he wanted to have a few last moments with his father. I asked him if he wanted me to leave for a few minutes, but he said no. He went up to the bed and stood directly across from me. I was completing my work, but I could tell he wanted to say something.

I was expecting him to say something like, "I am really going to miss my father. He was a great dad," or maybe, "I can't believe he's gone." Instead, he started to talk, and as I looked up at him across his dead father's bed, he said, "Hey, Tia, do you think maybe you and I could go out for a coffee or something?"

Your dad just died and you are asking me out? I thought. *What the hell!* I gave him a little silence while trying to think of what to say. Then I said, "No." This "no" meant "not only will I not go out with you," but also, "you just did a real weird thing."

Then I told him that I appreciated the offer, but that my life was just too busy at the moment. I don't know why I said that, but I suppose I was thinking that it was still my job to keep peace at this horrible moment of a death.

The sister came to the door and called him into the other room. Soon after, I heard the front door open and then close. I was glad. I finished my work and went into the living room. The brother was gone. As it turned out, the sister had heard him ask me out. She said that she was so sorry for what her idiot brother had done. I told her not to worry about it.

We finished our business, and I waited with her for the people who would come and get the body. I have learned that no one wants to be alone in a house with a dead body, even if it is a family member, so I always try to stay with the family until this gets done.

I used to think that it was always nice to get asked out, but after this situation, I have to say that I now have one exception.

After this visit, I headed to a meeting at work about the pending protests.

I went into the meeting, and all the top dogs were there. This was a preparedness meeting for possible civil unrest. It was announced that we would most likely receive a twenty-four-hour advance warning. We were told that we would need to keep our phones on day and night. We were further instructed to make sure all of our patients had medical and personal supplies in their homes. As we reviewed the list of supplies, the speaker singled me out and asked if I could think of anything else.

No one was surprised by this, because everyone knew that I had been preparing for weeks. I told them that they needed to keep their own personal supplies in their vehicles, of course. I also said they should develop a personal exit plan. I added that, besides food and water, they would need to ensure that the family had a can opener and candles. A lot of people do not normally eat canned food, and thus do not necessarily have a manual can opener available in case the electric goes out. I also advised the group that we needed to supply patients who require it with oxygen tanks in case the power goes out. I reminded them that recently the bad people had figured out how to turn off power for whole neighborhoods. In fact, this had just happened on the previous night in Ferguson.

As the meeting went on, we discussed how having a security person along may not be enough, because there could be crowds or gangs of people out there who could easily overcome us. The plan was to treat the civil unrest like a major snowstorm.

Other conversations centered on how widespread the potential unrest might be. The hotspot had been determined to be, of course, Ferguson, and the surrounding adjacent communities, but there had also been a good deal of protesting and unrest in the downtown St. Louis area. To the surprise of a lot of people in the room, we also discussed the Clayton area. There had been a lot of protests there because that is where the St. Louis County Prosecuting Attorney had his office. Some protesters had worked to get him off the case and might blame him if there turned out to be no trial for the police officer.

The Shaw neighborhood of St. Louis was also added to the list of potential trouble spots because there had been a lot of protesting in that area recently.

It was interesting to watch all of the attendees as they realized that basically most of the city and county was of concern. I already knew this, being aware of the concern about shots fired recently—even on the highways that encircle and cut through the city.

Others mentioned that they knew a number of individuals boarding up their businesses in areas that seemed far away from Ferguson but that might also turn out to be targets.

Our security personnel talked about what we should do and made sure everyone knew they could call them at any time, day or night. Our security company had boarded up their facility also. We were instructed not to go to the office after dark, for fear that some may think we kept drugs at the facility, which we do not.

We ended the meeting, and there was a TV on in the other office where the governor of Missouri and several law enforcement officials were giving speeches about all the recent additional training they had participated in. They also emphasized that they were ready to ensure peaceful protesting, but added that they were prepared to handle any civil unrest as well.

Many of my co-workers seemed a little shocked by all the preparedness activities that were transpiring. They seemed most alarmed that there just didn't seem to be many safe areas throughout the city where they could feel comfortable. This was an eye opener for them.

So we waited. I hoped and prayed that nothing would happen, and I really didn't know which way the verdict would go. I realized that if the case did not result in charges or a trial, all of the concern about unrest and civil disturbances was well founded. I also thought of the unfortunate families who were in the process of experiencing the death of a loved one, and thought it a shame that we might not be able to provide them with first-class care.

"Check yourself before you wreck yourself."
—*Tina*

CHAPTER 25

I Smell Gas and It Isn't Coming from the Patient

As we moved toward the end of November, there was still no grand jury announcement. I started my day as usual one morning, rolling into Starbucks and greeting the regulars. I bought my cup of coffee and green tea and set up my shop at my reserved spot at the breakfast bar. I looked at my schedule for the day, stepped outside, and started calling my patients to set up visit times and security, if needed. Back inside, I looked over and noticed the local paper on the table behind me.

I always checked the headlines to find out what had happened the night before. Depending on what the news was, it could alter my plans for the day. Wow! St. Louis had been ranked fourth in the country for having the highest crime rate. The article about this noted that by the end of October 2014, there had already been 120 murders—which is more than the total for all of 2013. This didn't surprise me.

Where I worked in North St. Louis, it seemed that there were at least one or more shootings daily and several murders each week.

My phone rang at that moment. It was the office calling to inform me that one of my patients had passed away. This particular patient had not been on my schedule for that day, but I always try to do the death visit for my patients' families when their loved one passes. A chaplain or social worker can also make the visit, but if all of my other patients are stable, I rearrange my schedule so that I can go. I feel that this is a good thing for the family and also for me, as we have been on a journey together, and being together for this final step seems appropriate and brings all of us closure. I called the family to offer my condolences by phone and to let them know I would be there in ten minutes.

Jessica, the patient's daughter, told me to take my time. This patient was middle aged and had been diagnosed just two months previously. She had five children ranging in age from twenty to thirty. I was on my way to a very rough area, but I did not take security because the patient's daughter was a fireman and always waited outside for me. She told me to never worry, that she had my back. I was only eight blocks from the patient's home.

I looked in my rearview mirror and saw two police Suburbans coming up behind me. *Whatever*, I thought to myself, *I have no warrant or traffic violations, and Lola is in fine condition.* They followed me all eight blocks. *Dudes, light 'em up, boys*, I thought. That was my slang for "pull me over if you really want to." They blasted on their lights as if they were chasing a bank robber and skidded in just behind me.

I pulled over right in front of the patient's home. *Really*, I thought. My patient's daughter, the firefighter, stood on the porch in her uniform watching the event with her brothers and seeming to enjoy the excitement. With all the noise, the crowd quickly grew to over twenty people, including the neighbors. *No problem, this will be quick*, I thought.

One of the officers walked to the front of the vehicle with his hand on his gun, while the other officer slowly walked up on my side. I had my hands on the steering wheel and knew not to reach for anything. The officer asked for my license and registration. I said, "Okay, my name is Tia and I am a nurse with a hospice company." I had my badge on, along with my scrubs, and there also was a medical bag in plain sight on the passenger seat.

He asked me where I was going. I pointed to the house we were parked in front of. I thought that this was somewhat amusing, but I didn't show it. The officer, however, didn't think it was funny. Then he said he needed to see my license and registration. I pulled it out and handed it to him. He didn't say anything but just went to his car. The other officer remained in front of my car.

I wasn't scared. I was a little embarrassed, though. I looked over to my left to see my patient's daughter standing in the yard with her nicely pressed blue fireman's uniform. She looked very confused. I waited fifteen minutes. Fifteen minutes! After the first five minutes, I was fuming. My patient had passed away, the family was waiting, and the policeman had not even asked me if there might be some kind of emergency.

Both of the cops could clearly see the family, and half the block was waiting in suspense. After ten minutes, my head cleared and I grew even more angry. Five minutes later, as I was about to lose it, the officer got out of his car and approached my window. He handed me my license and registration and told me to have a nice day.

Have a nice day! I thought. Now *that* pissed me off. *Why don't you say something like, "Sorry, we thought you were a hooker, and we're real glad that you aren't and that you are a nurse doing your job with an almost perfect driving record."?* "Have a nice day" meant to me, "Shit, we thought we caught somebody, but she's a goddamn real nurse and now we look kind of stupid, so we are going to just act like nothing happened and not be nice to her because she didn't turn out to be a criminal."

So I got ready to let them know how pissed off I was, not because I got pulled over, but because they weren't nice about it. I mustered a little nerve and said, "Why did you pull me over?" That's not what I wanted to say, but I didn't want to go to jail on that day.

The officer told me that my license-plate frame was obstructing the month that indicates when my plates expire. I felt better for a moment, but soon was fuming again. I had to "check myself before I wrecked myself."

I have a Washington Redskins license-plate frame cover. I have had this while living in five different states over the past nine years and have never been pulled over for it—it had never been a problem before. I was getting ready to say, "What, you got a problem with the Redskins?" That's the nicest thing I could think of to say, but since it wasn't a good day to die, I just said, "You have a nice day, too."

This was lame, but since he didn't even tell me to change out the frame, I knew I got pulled over because I was white.

I know a lot of police officers and almost all of them are great. I have a massive amount of respect for what they do. I have relatives who were in law enforcement, and several of my friends have family members who are police officers.

What happened that day had been so unlike all my other experiences with police officers. All the other times, there had been mutual respect. When an officer pulls over a doctor, nurse, fireman, EMT or other public servant, there is usually candid conversation. As a nurse, I had always been treated with great respect.

There were a few other times when I had been pulled over in the neighborhood because the police were concerned about my safety. On occasion, they would offer to follow me to my destination—but not this day.

They had profiled me. I'm okay with that, but they didn't need to act like assholes when they found out they were wrong. I do know now how it feels to not only get profiled, but also to experience the attitude that goes along with it. It was only once, but I will always remember it.

I got out of the car, grabbed my medical bag and walked through the crowd smiling, but I let them all wonder what had just happened. Maybe they were happy because I am white and I got pulled over. Maybe they knew me and they were angry with me. The daughter gave me a hug on the porch. "They better not have given you a ticket," she said. My patient's other sons were laughing. I told them that I hadn't gotten a ticket.

"You know why you were pulled over, don't you?" said one of the sons. "First of all, there was just a guy shot dead in the street this morning before you got here. Second, you are a little blonde chick driving a bright-red Audi in the hood. The cops thought you were a prostitute or buying drugs. Your badge and uniform could be a front."

I gave the boys a hug, greeted the other family members and friends in the living room and went in the bedroom to see my patient. A little while later, we all went on the porch and talked about the wonderful life their mother had lived and how blessed I had been to take care of her.

Soon I left, and as I was driving away and thinking about the family, I knew they would be alright. They were a close family. It was just so sad that they had lost their mother. I was thinking about my own mother who had survived the same illness and was doing great. My family had been very lucky, but I knew that this family was strong and I was confident that over time, they, too, would be just fine.

I went on my way to the next patient. She was a rather large woman, bedridden and pretty old. Her son, who was also older and in poor health, was her caregiver. They lived in a beautiful four-story home in the heart of my territory. I called him to let the son know that I was on my way. I was in a hurry but was very careful not to speed. I definitely did not want to get pulled over again.

The son always needed to know exactly when I would arrive because it took him about ten minutes to get from the upstairs down the spiral staircase to the front door, and it took another five minutes to unlock all of the various locks on the door. He told me he did not want me to wait outside because the neighborhood was so unsafe.

As I left my car and did my look-around thing, there seemed to be a familiar odor in the air. The home was very close to the street. As I stepped onto the front porch, the smell of gas hit me. I opened the unlocked front door and almost passed out from the fumes. I didn't knock because I realized there would not be time for formalities. I hustled into the bedroom where the patient was lying in her bed, her son lying next to her.

"Wake up! We need to go outside right now!" I shouted as I shook them awake. "There's a gas leak!"

The son seemed groggy. "I'm too tired, please let me just get some rest."

As the son slowly started to get up and move outside, I heard some noise from the kitchen. I ran in there and there was a young woman standing there. I recognized her—she came in from time to time to cook and clean and watch the patient.

"Get out of the house immediately!" I told her. "There's a gas leak, don't you smell it? Call 911!"

"No, let me just finish up," she said. I grabbed her by the arm and led her in the direction of the front door that I had left open. The son had come back inside and was trying to move his mother, but he did not have enough strength to get her out of bed.

I looked at my patient and wondered how I would ever get her out of the house. I am strong for my size, but she made two of me. I ran into the other room to get the wheelchair but I had to collapse it to pass it through the doorway. I soon realized that this idea would not work.

"Shit!" I said. The gas was so concentrated that I could feel it having an effect on me. I also knew that just a small flicker of flame, or perhaps someone hitting an electrical switch, could blow up the house with us in it.

Finally, I grabbed a wooden chair from across the room and somehow got her into it. Then I dragged it across the carpet, trying to balance her the whole time as she almost fell off every time I pulled the chair a few feet. We arrived outside on the porch at last.

"Did anyone call 911?" I yelled. What is cool about emergencies is that you can yell and cuss and people think you are the one in charge.

By now the neighbors were coming out of their houses. No one said anything except "what's going on," so I called 911 myself. We got my patient to the sidewalk. I watched the mother and son coming back to life. I listened to them complain about how hot it was, so I knew they were doing okay. It was about ninety degrees, and the adrenaline was finally leaving my system. I began to feel somewhat better.

Then came the police, an ambulance, a fire truck and a fancy white utility company truck. At that moment, I loved all those people—even the police. Man, it looked and sounded like they were pulling over a white blonde chick for a covered-up license-plate frame!

They all glanced at me and at the mother and son on the sidewalk. I felt they knew who I was. As they went in and then came out, they had that "Oh Shit" look on their faces. Along with the EMTs, I attended to the patient, the son and the well-meaning helper. They didn't look well. All three of them had actually gone to sleep in the chairs we had brought down off the porch. We kept them awake and did our thing.

Relaxed a little, I simply felt thankful that everyone was okay.

The man from the gas company walked up to me and reported that there had been an open gas pipe in the basement and that we were all very lucky. The son overheard him and told us that his cousin had just been over to remove the gas dryer from their basement. The utility man said that he'd failed to cap off the gas line.

The cousin just shook his head; he couldn't imagine anyone doing that. Hell, I couldn't imagine anyone doing such a thing, either. You would smell and hear the gas immediately. The utility man said he had also found another slow leak that he'd fixed.

He asked me who I was and I told him. He said, "Did you call us?" I said, "Yes." He winked at me. He smiled at my patient, then the son, and then grabbed his tools and headed for his truck. He didn't tell me to "have a nice day." I thought he was a nice man.

CHAPTER 26

White People Have a Different Rule

I had been so exhausted from the gas-leak events that I came home and went straight to bed. This gave me a little quality time with my kittens. They love attention. I got up a bit early the next day, so I was able to take my time getting ready for work. It was a Friday, and I didn't have to work on the weekend. All I had planned for the day was a long meeting at the office and a few regular visits.

A message popped up on the computer to check out the local news and weather. One story reported that the attorney general was pleased with some of the changes being implemented by the local officials in Ferguson. He had previously commented that he thought there needed to be an "overhaul of the local police." One of the heads of the local police department observed that the attorney general had not even met with them when he'd come into town.

There were comments from all the local and state politicians. Everyone was concerned about the potential civil unrest that could occur over the next few days when the announcement about the grand jury decision would most likely be made.

I read another story about how applications for concealed carry had doubled from the previous year in the area. The reporters had interviewed an elderly woman who had bought a gun and was applying for her concealed-carry permit. She seemed like an ordinary woman who simply wanted to protect herself. It was sad to me that she felt she had to do this.

I already had the TV on and I was listening to some footage of an interview reporters had done with a former chief of police. He had a concern with how the police might respond to future criminal activity in the community. He explained that, with all the people coming down on what they referred to as "excessive force," the police may hold back in situations where they had once been aggressive. He offered an example where the police had seen some unusual activity in a dark alley late at night in a residential area. In the past, he explained, the police would take a proactive stance and approach the individuals involved to determine what might be happening. He suggested that, with all the criticism of their techniques, they would back off more, becoming more passive and hesitant to intervene in some crime situations. I was thinking that this might be what some people in the community were asking for.

I finished getting ready and went off to my meeting at the office. Since I was a bit early, I went into the lunchroom and ran into one of my favorite people—a fantastic nurse named Emma. All of our nurses are pretty damned good, but this one is great, and I had tremendous respect for her. She does what I do, but she does it on the night shift.

Emma once told me she had been raised in the projects, and I could tell that she was very street wise. We normally didn't get to visit much because she was on a different shift.

"I went to see one of your patients last night," she said, smiling. "I never worry about anything when I go to visit one of your patients because I know you take great care of them, and they all love you. It was an admission visit and they wanted to know if I would be taking care of them," she went on. "I told them not to worry, that Tia would be coming. I told them that Tia is a short, blonde, white girl, but they need to just give you a chance and you will do a great job."

I told Emma how much I appreciated that, because I know they trusted her and believed what she said. "It means a lot to me that you said that," I told her, "It saves me time in building their trust and getting them on my side."

Then she said, "Tia, you really love what you do, don't you?"

"I do. The territory I have is kind of like my home," I replied. "I do my job. I go home and eat and sleep, then I go back to work. Once a year I treat myself to a football trip where my buddy and I are trying to visit all the NFL stadiums in our lifetime."

Emma and I finished our visit in the lunchroom, and as we were finishing up our snacks, she dropped a big hunk of her cookie on the floor. This wasn't any old cookie. It was one of those two-dollar cookies that are the size of your hand with nuts poking out in between the giant chunks of chocolate chips. She picked it up and looked at me, smiling. "You white people have a 'three-second rule,'" she teased. "Black people don't have any limit." She smiled mischievously as she took a healthy bite of the cookie.

We laughed together and she patted me on the back as we left the lunchroom.

This kind of conversation—one that casually or teasingly mentions race—might be uncomfortable for some people in some workplaces, but it is common with the people I work with and it works for us. I think that because we all have so much respect for one another, we can speak openly and freely. Some say that this is the same kind of communication that exists in combat situations and on many sports teams. We actually do life and death work, and we are all on the same team.

We are all in the same foxhole, so to speak, and we share that bond. We are dependent on one another and we want to get along. I think that is why it works.

In the meeting that morning, we were informed that the grand jury announcement should happen the following Sunday. Our supervisors described how the hospital systems were all working together to handle any potential overflow. We were told how, in order to avoid potential conflicts, emergency responders had even developed plans to send injured protesters to one hospital and police injuries to another.

One speaker informed us that there was a National Guard presence at the airport, in Clayton, downtown, North St. Louis, the Shaw neighborhood, and of course, Ferguson. They went on to say that the police had designated a group to handle all the 911 calls separately from dealing with the protesters. This had been a problem during the initial protesting and rioting.

The meeting ended and my mind drifted toward my own plans should civil unrest come closer. I would be flying out to California that week to meet my friend, and we would be visiting a couple of new stadiums. He is a great guy and we had been doing this for years. Apart from my work, these trips were really the highlight of my life.

My plan was to take my kitties to my parents' home on Tuesday night. They loved to watch them and their home was located safely across the river in another state. With the cats safe, I planned to drive to the airport and leave Lola there for my return. I had thought about taking a cab, but then I wouldn't have the car there at the airport and might not be able to get to my parents' home safely when I returned on Monday to pick up the kitties. While I live in a relatively safe area, I thought that it might not be wise to drive there amid the uncertainty of the protests, possible road closures, etc.

My friend and I had planned to go to a Thursday night game in Oakland, then to San Francisco for a Sunday game. I had once worked in Oakland, and that place is pretty unsafe itself. In fact, my buddy and I were planning to wear Oakland jerseys just so we didn't get attacked. In Oakland, they separate the Oakland fans from the opposing team fans to reduce the violence. We weren't Oakland fans, but we were smart fans.

Oakland has some pretty tough areas. When I worked there, I remembered driving to the hospital where I worked the first day. I saw my exit sign and took the turn off the highway. I got to the bottom of the exit and found myself in a bad area. It looked like a war zone. I was immediately pulled over by the police. I rolled down my window and they asked me what the hell I was doing there.

I told them about the exit sign I had taken, and they informed me that the criminals often moved the signs to get unsuspecting people to take the wrong exit, and then they would rob them or worse. I got the hell out of there and went to work. There were police and security guards all over the place at the hospital. They provided all the nurses with a security escort. It was a rough place.

I was also thinking about a news story that I had read about nationwide plans for all of the protesting related to the grand jury decision. Apparently the protest leaders had instructed the protesters to go to a designated site to protest at 5 p.m. on the day of the announcement or the next day at 5 p.m. if the announcement was made after 5 p.m. The story indicated that this was taking place in all major cities, so it occurred to me that possibly no major city would be perfectly safe.

Like many people, I just wanted it all to be over so that I could go back to my normal, crazy life.

Later that week I got up early and dressed up a bit more than usual. I was going to see a doctor with the mother of one of my best friends. My friend lived in California with her two beautiful children, so I was filling in for her with her parents who lived in town.

I loved her parents, and they always treated me like family. I had known them since their daughter and I were in college, which was about fifteen years ago. They lived nearby, so I go and see them from time to time.

Recently, I had gone to several doctor visits with the wife to assist her while she went through cancer treatments. It had been rough for her, but she is a strong person and we were all looking for a great outcome. I really like her, and I love watching her interact with her husband. She is a very caring person, a great mother and grandmother. The husband, too, is a character. I just love to visit with him. He is in good shape and walks about three miles every day. He calls me kiddo. The husband and wife love each other dearly, and they have really comical, entertaining arguments.

While the wife was going through her cancer treatments, her husband had an episode that sent him to the doctor. They immediately called me to get my help. We met at the doctor's office to find out what the doctors planned to do. It turned out that he would have to go into the hospital for an operation—news that was no surprise—and the outcome looked very promising.

I usually don't talk much while the doctors are speaking, because I don't want to interfere. I had come there for moral support. As it turned out, the doctors set the operation for the day I would be leaving for my trip. My friend's parents thus decided to call in their oldest son, who lived nearby. Normally this would not be a problem, but he was a policeman who had been on twenty-four-hour call because of all the protests and unrest. The parents decided not to tell my best friend who lived in California. They did not want her to worry or to cause her to jump on a plane with her two children.

With all of this, I was a little stressed. The mother was being treated for cancer and the father was going to have heart surgery. I couldn't tell my best friend—their daughter—what was going on, the riots were ready to break out, and I was leaving town the day of the operation. Basically, I couldn't talk to my best friend about all my problems, because she might have asked me about her parents and I would have had to lie.

Nurses are constantly asked for advice and help with medical issues from family members and friends. With our education, experience and contacts, we can do a lot of good in these circumstances. I also try to serve as a calming influence with the people I assist.

Watching my friend's mother go through her cancer fight took me back to the fight my own mother put up with her cancer ordeal. She had been diagnosed with late-stage ovarian cancer. In a way, my mother was a hero to me. She did all the usual hard things mothers do as they raise their children. She is a very tough, honest and healthy person. When we got the news, we were all shocked, because she is middle aged and we didn't really have a history of this sort of cancer in our family.

I went to my father for certain things over the years because he was a businessman and a handyman. He just knows a great deal about a lot of things, and he has connections. I depended on my mom for many things, especially the relationship stuff.

For years I watched my mom as she took in stray dogs and eventually found them homes. She didn't give them to just anybody. She would interview the family and then drive by and inspect the family's home and yard to assure herself that the animal would have a good home.

I watched my mother go through life-threatening cancer. It was confusing and difficult for me at the time as I was living halfway across the country. I was troubled by a variety of questions and concerns. *Should I go home or just help from afar? How do you help from so far away? Do I get intimately involved in all the medical issues, or just try to be a supportive daughter?*

Ultimately, I was able to do both. My father tapped in to me and my professional sources. With the help of many of my doctor friends, we got the best physician for my mother and developed a great care plan. Once we had things in place, my father told me to it was time to just be a daughter.

Living through my mother's cancer experience has given me a great deal of empathy in relating to the family members of the dying patient. I know the fear of not knowing what is going to happen and the feeling of helplessness to control outcomes. We put our faith in the doctors and their team.

I consider myself a person of action, but when my mother was diagnosed, I was too messed up to be of much help. I still feel guilty about this when I have patients who have the same kind of cancer, especially when I know the outcome is not promising. I know the pain of waiting for what seems like forever for test results. There is no quick resolution, and sometimes there is a chance of the cancer coming back.

People who have survived cancer, including my mom, tell me that no matter what the doctors tell them, they always live with the fear of the cancer returning. Cancer Sucks!

Over the years, I have gained even more respect for my mother as I have watched others go through similar situations.

I learned that you can be there for these people, but they really must face it alone. They are facing death, and you are not. We can't really understand what this is like or totally relate to it. I do know that in every case the survivors are different people when they emerge. They almost always appreciate life more and no longer sweat the small stuff.

It was a new day as I headed to the airport for my football vacation. I prayed the heart operation went well for my best friend's father. I hoped that all of my patients were going to be okay, and I hoped the city would not be burned down when I returned.

CHAPTER 27

Ferguson Burns

Just two hours after the announcement of "no trial," I watched at least twelve businesses burn to the ground in Ferguson, Missouri. Michael Brown's stepfather was seen on TV telling an angry crowd to "Burn the motherfucker down!" and "Burn this bitch down!" The police reported over 150 gunshots fired. Protesters shut down highways. Businesses were looted. There were over sixty arrests, most of them citizens of Ferguson. These events were covered on all TV channels, local and nationwide. My phone was ringing off the hook and Facebook was full of reactions.

There were protests planned in all of the major cities and more planned for the next day. I received my alerts from work warning us to check in before we went on any visits. John called me with an update, and many other people called me to make sure I was alright.

Although I lived by myself, I stayed in close contact with my family and friends. The kitties were at my parents' house. I had two exit plans. The first was that my father and brother would come and get me and take me to my parents' house. The other was that I would head west to my former supervisor's house. She had offered to take me in. Finally, if those two plans did not pan out, I felt safe because one of my best friends and her family lived just a half-block away. I knew I could run down there in a minute. I stayed glued to the TV and internet, with the cell phone in my ear. Everything I thought would happen—but hoped wouldn't—was happening and happening fast.

That town was burning down! And when the fire department arrived at the fires, they had to turn around and leave because of the bullets flying over their heads. Giant fire hoses were abandoned in the street. Someone threw firebombs into a row of cars which burned, one by one. Two police cars were burned to the ground. Ten more patrol cars were damaged. An officer was shot in the arm in another part of the city. Sixteen people were treated for injuries. And, it may have been related to the rioting or not, a dead body was found in a burning car.

One man was carjacked and then run over by the thieves. The clergy members who had tried to keep the peace during the August riots were not around. One of the protesters was interviewed. He was from the south side of the city and his group had just shut down the highway. He said they would move to another location. The police followed them with a "prisoner bus." The protester told the TV reporter that his group was not responsible for breaking the storefront glass and looting. He said that, in fact, while the group was out in front protesting, cars full of people had pulled up and individuals got out, broke the glass and began to loot the businesses.

A sense of déjà vu came over me. The rioting, chaos, and devastation looked similar to what initially had taken place in August, only this time it seemed more widespread and destructive. Also, the same as last time, it appeared the police were backing off. This was very hard to watch. I wondered how those business owners were feeling as they watched their businesses being burned and destroyed, and no one was doing anything about it.

I had just returned home from my trip a couple of hours before I watched Ferguson burn and later found out that all inbound flights had been cancelled a short time after I arrived. I was tired. I had really thought that a few days of vacation would get me away from the turmoil in the city. As it turned out, most people I spoke with while on vacation were following the events unfolding in Ferguson and wanted to discuss it with me because I was close to the situation. Ferguson was also in the newspapers and on the TV monitors in the airports.

The trip itself had been great. My good friend and I knocked off two of the stadiums on our list. We went to games at Levi Stadium in San Francisco and a game in Oakland, California. The Redskins lost again, but I still loved them. What made the trip special was that my friend's girlfriend met us for the second game.

This was the first time she had come on one of our stadium trips. We had met before, but I really never had a chance to get to know her. She was so awesome—she loves football and she loves my friend. While on the trip, they informed me that they were getting married. I was so happy about this. It made the trip even better. We watched football, we ate, we drank, we laughed, we caught up on family stuff, and most important, we made plans for the other twenty-three stadiums we needed to visit next.

We have now been to Sun Devil Stadium in Arizona, Fed Ex Stadium in Baltimore, Maryland, what I call the Dallas Palace, Lucas Oil Stadium in Indianapolis, Indiana, Met Life Stadium in New Jersey, and just recently, Oakland and San Francisco. We have been to other stadiums, but not together, so those don't count. We also had a blast creating our plans for next year.

Those good times faded quickly as I watched all of the breaking news. My mind turned to my patients and their families. How were they feeling as they watched this city erupt? Although I would be off work the next day, I was anxious to check in on them when I returned to work.

My patients were dying and they and their families had to witness all of this. Many of them were in or close to ground zero. *What would tomorrow bring?* I wondered. Protests were planned in 115 cities in thirty-seven states. The grand jury decision had tapped into a vein of rage and blood was flowing. All of this seemed so sad and tragic.

"I'm so glad that I know more than I knew then
Gonna keep on tryin'
'Till I reach my highest ground."
—*Stevie Wonder, Higher Ground*

CHAPTER 28
Two Weeks of Hell

On the first day back to work after my vacation, I started my day from home as I always do. I checked my computer for my assignments and then made the phone calls to set them up. It's hard to go back to work after a vacation, but I did look forward to seeing all my patients and their families. Almost all of my patients didn't want to see anyone but me, so many of them had waited until I got back from vacation instead of calling in for another staff member. My boss and some of my co-workers also liked this, because they would often need to arrange for security if they were to see one of my patients.

Off on my calls I went, and it was like a series of homecomings. They were all as happy to see me as I was to see them. They wanted to know every detail about my trip, as if they were living vicariously through me. They seemed truly happy for me. It was all I could do to turn the conversation back around to them, but that was my job and why I was there.

I was tired from being on vacation, but I felt rejuvenated after seeing my patients. I popped by the office for some supplies, and while there, my boss asked to see me in her office. *Okay*, I thought, *she is going to welcome me back*. Without providing a lot of detail, I can tell you that I was being called out on something that

I had done at work. The company viewed it as a serious issue. I was provided with the information and informed that I could submit a challenge.

At that moment, my world of friends, football, patients, and my love for what I do all seemed in jeopardy. I suffered for the next two weeks, waiting for the final outcome. I barely slept or ate. My cats were at my parents' house, so I was alone at home. My father was out in the woods harvesting deer. I usually call him and my mom for advice, and this would be the first time I had to deal with a situation like this alone. I had been through difficult situations such as this before over the years, but it was the "doing it alone" part that really sucked. Every time things like this happen, you think the world is going to end, even if it never does. My imagination raced through scenarios of the worst possible outcome and I felt that it was going to be horrible.

I told a few of my friends outside of work about what was taking place, and to my great relief, they offered me tremendous support—the real kind of support that helps you to stand up and go into action. As I saw my patients over the next two weeks, they also offered me support, even though they had no idea of what was going on. They seemed even more precious to me than ever during this time. They are why I do what I do, and I don't want anyone or anything keeping me from taking care of them. I imagined my life without them and it wasn't a life that I wanted.

My father later reminded me of what he always says when these things happen. He worked for thirty-five years in the business world, and he saw it all. He offered me these lessons learned:

He told me that sometimes you are just wrong, and you have to provide an honest and complete defense. Then you live with the results.

He taught me that good employees will get into trouble from time to time. This is expected.

He said that being a great employee is not a defense.

He told me that, like most people, I would most likely have a problem at least once a year or every couple years on average and at the end of the day, it is how I handle it that matters.

He reminded me again about the Richard Pryor movie scene where Richard Pryor comes home to his wife after quitting a job that he hated. Richard and his wife had planned how he would tell the bosses off and then quit the job. He wanted some satisfaction. So Richard went to work. He came home upset and says to his wife, "I gave them the wrong finger." The lesson is that if you're going to quite a job, do it right.

My father also taught me to take full responsibility when wrong—and to do so immediately.

He always said if you are not in the wrong, fight to the death unless you have no respect for the company.

We have fought a few battles together and have a great record. In fact, now he sometimes asks *me* for advice.

I knew it was time to go out on my own. I was preparing for battle. The company wasn't the enemy and my boss wasn't the problem. The level of discipline was what I needed to address.

Possibly, you, the reader, may have gone through this type of trying situation yourself or perhaps you have seen a friend or family member go through it. While going through these tough times, it is difficult to believe that it will ever be over. There is always a feeling of helplessness. If any bosses are reading this, maybe you can pick up a tip or two on how to handle these situations in a more humane manner.

One thing a good boss will do is move quickly, and I appreciated that my company did this. For the employee, as the hours and days drag on, waiting for an outcome can be like waiting for cancer screening results: like torture. Even though this ultimately did not apply in my case, bosses should talk at length to the potential offender before dropping the bomb on them. And they should have all the facts to ensure that the employee has been given due process. It is also important to administer penalties consistently and fairly, ensuring that all the rules have been clear and the level of punishment or discipline established for the various levels of offenses.

I dedicated a good deal of time to preparing my defense, grateful to have lots of supportive friends. I was not able to sleep or eat much. I had, in fact, done something wrong. I admitted this in the initial meeting. I know better than to have done what I did, but the punishment did not fit the crime, in my view. With my friends behind me and some very strong, hot coffee, I went to work and penned a six-page document to turn in. God, I felt better after I wrote that. The document was entirely truthful, including my admission of guilt.

I turned in my defense and went into that "waiting period" thing. The truth is that I was pretty confident that I would be okay, but as my father always said, "strange things can happen to good employees." We have all seen it. I love my job, but I know I could get another job the next day. That wasn't the issue. The issue was that I love what I do, I love my company, I love the people I work with—and I don't want to do anything else.

During the waiting period, my friends called me, texted me and emailed me. I learned from them how to be a great friend if it ever happens to one of them. I will never forget their support.

The days dragged on. Although I was still not sleeping or eating well, my patients kept me busy. I have definitely learned my lesson on what I did wrong. I have admitted it to my company and to myself, and it has been forever engraved in my brain. The company was right about their position and I had no issue with that. My goal was to have the punishment fit the crime.

A few days later, I went to the office and asked if I could visit with my supervisors or if another time would be better. I had a sense of urgency and wanted to just get it over with. So we talked and I was told that the original punishment of "my life as I knew it being destroyed" had been revised to "a note in my file that we had a conversation about my infraction." I broke down and cried. They seemed concerned at this and asked me what I was thinking. I looked up and said, "This is what I thought should have taken place from the beginning." I told them that I was crying because I was relieved and just glad it was over. This was not what most people would have said or should have said. It just came out. I'm not sure what they even thought I meant by it, it was just how I felt. If you ever find yourself in a similar situation, it would probably not be wise to say what I did. I have no regrets, though. I am human, and in a way, I hope that they appreciated my honesty.

In the end, I was treated fairly, and I learned from my mistake. Most important, I handled it myself with a little help from my friends.

My family always celebrates these types of victories with food. I am usually a health nut when it comes to eating, but I headed for the nearest Wendy's restaurant—a true departure for me. I ordered a burger with everything on it, some greasy french fries, and one of those "Frosty" frozen shakes. Like a starving man who has just been found in the middle of the woods and fed for the first time in weeks, I was only able to choke about half of it down, but I felt great.

My phone was blowing up with calls from my friends. It was a welcome sound.

CHAPTER 29

The Flames Spread from Ferguson

Not long after the Michael Brown grand jury decision, I went about my daily routine and stopped to reflect on how the incident in Ferguson had spread across the entire United States—and even beyond.

One day as I was in the office, I heard a yell from across the room. It was my friend, Shanna. We met in the middle of the room and hugged. She seemed excited about something, and I was anxious for her to tell me what was on her mind. She asked me if I had heard about the kids bringing guns to school at two of the metropolitan area's more upscale high schools. I told her that I had indeed heard about that. She told me how pissed off she was, because she and her husband were working very hard to pay so that her children could go to school in a "nice" area. They were an African-American family, and she had taken her son out of the Ferguson schools because of all the problems. "Now it turns out that kids are bringing guns into the rich white kids' schools," she said, shaking her head. "I just can't believe it happened."

We kind of laughed together, but we were both disappointed that her family's sacrifice wasn't foolproof. I tried to reassure her by telling her that the school would clamp down and that her kids were still better off there.

I headed back out on the streets again, thinking about how my friend had struggled to create a good life for her children. I thought about the burned and now-boarded-up local businesses that had employed many community residents as workers. These workers now had no jobs. It was weird to think that this nationwide issue had begun in the streets that I drove through daily. There were so many good people and families whose struggles had, as a result of these conflicts, grown worse.

As Ferguson attempted to get back to some sense of normalcy, several major cities across the United States flared up with racial tension and unrest. Once the two police officers were murdered in New York City, it seemed that the war had been defined. This war would be the police against the African Americans. As in all wars, most people are innocent. Usually the leaders and the media create the wars, fan the flames, and keep them going. Usually they have something to gain from this.

I noted that most of the black-on-white, black-on-black, and white-on-white police situations had been festering for some time. What seems to have changed is that the news media now reports on each and every incident, sometimes manufacturing or misrepresenting the story line or capturing only a few select facts to present the story in a predetermined way. And then the public officials and politicians milk it for votes.

Most of the statistics don't show increases in these types of encounters, but from viewing television or following the web-based news reports, the general public may come to believe that there has been a dramatic increase. I know this perception has occurred locally in St. Louis and nationally with increased attention to shootings by police as well as police officers being shot.

The media talking heads have opined that race relations have been set back forty years. It seemed to me that, if you listened to some people in high places, there had been an effort to create an environment that gives that impression. I pondered what the average white person and average black person thought of all of this. Those were the opinions that interested me.

In my world, the white people I know—yes, I have some white friends—have been surprised to hear about the issues being highlighted. They tend to go about their daily lives without considering race relations much, and they seem to believe that relations with African Americans have improved. They believe that they personally have not intentionally done anything to harm African Americans. Do they or should they be doing things to help black communities? Some feel guilty that they aren't doing anything specific.

Of course, I am white. I know that even though I spend half of my waking life with African Americans, they may not always be totally candid with me. Just for fun, let's assume that they are. Generally, most of those who have volunteered information about race relations have a similar opinion to mine. The mothers, grandmothers and fathers I talk to just want their kids to have a better life than they did. They work hard to teach their kids to do the right thing. They want their kids to attend good schools and to get good jobs. Several have told me that they fear some of the young African-American men in the neighborhood. There are locks on the doors and bars on the windows. This is to keep out the young African-American troublemakers. They have been candid with me about that. Yes, there are a lot of bad young white men also, and other whites and some African Americans fear them as well.

There doesn't seem to be much hope in their eyes when they talk about the future. I also share that feeling. I have not seen good solutions and good leadership. They can hope and I can hope that it will get better.

In speaking with older African Americans, they have communicated to me that they are happy with the progress that has been made. These are individuals who have seen real racial ugliness. Many of them experienced it firsthand and described to me how much better things are now. In my view, they are certainly not saying that race relations are the way they should be, but only that there has been improvement and in general, things are so much better.

My mind wandered on this subject as I made my way to one of my patient's homes. This was a really lovely family. The daughter always looked out for me, so I had decided not to take security along. As I turned the corner to roll up to the house, a truck suddenly pulled alongside my car and slammed on its brakes. I swerved toward the curb and was trapped as the truck swerved with me.

This is the end of my life, I thought. *What was I thinking when I decided to do this job?* It occurred to me that this scene would be how things might end for me. Then things grew worse. The guy in the truck began to scream at me. I was so frightened that I couldn't tell what he was trying to say. I was so fearful that I understood what it means to be almost "scared to death."

I had always tried to avoid getting hemmed in with my vehicle and briefly considered using my car as a weapon. I had talked to many people about that, but there was no opportunity to floor the gas on Lola and escape. I looked down the street and caught sight of Shandra, the daughter of my patient, running in my direction and yelling at the driver.

I cracked the passenger-side window down to see what the crazy guy in the truck was trying to say.

"Hey, I was just checking to see if you were okay!" he shouted.

At this point, I could hear Shandra yelling at him. "Get the fuck out of here!" she screamed.

Man, was I glad that she was my friend and had been looking out for me. She continued to scream and her shouts grew louder and louder as she cussed out the man in the truck. Her tirade was like poetry flowing from her lips. In fact, I learned a few combinations of curse-words that I hadn't heard before. I think, to be effective in this area, you need to be able to yell cuss words non-stop until the threat is removed, and Shandra was very skillful at this. She also swung her arms and beat her fist in the air. Any human being would have feared that woman. The guy in the truck shrugged and drove off, still trying to explain himself to Shandra, who couldn't hear this because she never stopped yelling. She stared him down as he retreated.

She came up to my car, mad as hell. "I can't believe that motherfucker was messing with you." She asked if I was okay and said she'd meet me at the house.

I realized that I had been naïve. I had really thought that I could handle most situations that might arise in my visiting area. I now know that I can't. My plan was not to use security when someone such as Shandra was looking out for me. That was stupid.

I got to the house, and Shandra was still mad as hell. She told me that the truck guy was familiar to her, and he could have really messed me up. I also think that she was embarrassed by the man's actions. I think she was embarrassed by the conduct of all the young African Americans who act that way, just as I am embarrassed by the way a lot of whites act.

She made sure I was okay, and we laughed for the next half-hour. I thought I was a strong woman, but my friend Shandra could easily have her picture in the dictionary next to "The African-American Terminator."

Shandra was one of the reasons I do what I do. She appreciated what I do and she wanted to help me as I cared for her mother.

That day, at that moment, she was truly my protector.

CHAPTER 30

Christmas and Hospice

Around the holidays, the number-one gift every family of mine prays for is that their dying family member will live through Christmas. I am asked on a daily basis by at least one of my patients' family members whether their relative will make it. I always tell them that I just don't know. We must say this in our business, even if we have an idea of when a patient will likely pass. I have been way off on my own unspoken predictions and have learned that no one can accurately predict exactly when a patient will pass.

I truly believe that dying patients can will themselves to live long enough to make it to Christmas or to that much-anticipated time when a child makes it home from another state, gets furloughed from prison or gets leave from the military. I have seen many cases where the doctor and I just cannot believe that some of my patients live as long as they do. Sometimes they defy the odds and live for days longer than expected—and sometimes months.

It was Christmas 2014. As I drove through the streets, I noticed that very few homes had decorations outside. Growing up, I was used to seeing them. This was different.

Some of the homes I visited were decorated inside and some were not. You can imagine how difficult it would be for a family with a dying loved one to muster the strength to get out all the decorations and put them up. What I have found is that families with small children and grandchildren usually find a way to get it accomplished. They do it for the kids, of course.

While the decorations aren't always displayed, two things always take place: Everyone gets all dressed up and goes to church, and then they come home and eat or go out to a great meal. The meals at home are usually huge. In each home, I often see enough food prepared to feed the entire neighborhood. They take a day off from any thought of healthy food and just cook all the stuff that tastes good.

During this year, one of my patients, Ron, found out I was scheduled to work on Christmas Day and he and his wife requested the exact time they wanted me to visit. When I told them I could make it happen, they said that this would be when they sat down for their Christmas meal, and they insisted that I be there. I loved this family. Ron and his wife, Becky, were wonderful and fun to be around. This patient was the one who had made a giant toolbox from a casket and had displayed it in his front yard.

I made the dinner date (I had a lunch hour coming anyway), but insisted that I do Ron's assessment before the festivities. Then we were off the clock. What a great time we had! How cool it was that they had invited me to this amazing banquet! We did not talk at all about dying or medicine. We ate and gave one another a hard time about whatever popped into our minds. I think this was the family's way of thanking me for the services and the friendship I provided them.

I also thought it possible that they felt sorry for me because I had to work on Christmas.

Actually, I like working on the holidays. With all the suffering I have seen, my view of Christmas has changed—I no longer become very excited about some of the superficial trappings of the holidays; these things seem shallow. My work itself—caring for people at the most vulnerable time of their lives—is what really has meaning for me and what Christmas is about. I enjoy giving my patients and their families comfort and making them happy, and they are all glad to see me on Christmas and treat me a little more special that day. Because my families usually have relatives visiting, I also get to meet many of the individuals I've heard about during the rest of the year.

After we ate our Christmas feast, we all went into the living room. Amidst all the presents and wrapping paper, I spotted a large red object in the corner—a miniature, bright-red, Audi toy car. It looked like Lola's little sister. The damned thing looked just like mine in the driveway, only smaller. I mean it *really* looked like mine. About that time, one of the granddaughters ran over and jumped in it, proclaiming, "We have the same cars!"

Ron had bought this little car for his granddaughter. I thought that this was incredibly cool. He said he had gone out to buy her a toy car, and there "mini-Lola" had been, sitting amongst the others. "It stood out from all the other models and colors and it reminded me of you," he said. "I knew I just had to get it. I told you I spoil my grandchildren, Tia."

We spent a little more time having fun and playing with the kids and then I had to be off to my next visit. I'd had such a great time, and reflected that this day had reminded me of why I love my work and why I don't mind working at Christmas. My patients are my Christmas.

While my patients are my true Christmas gift, we do sometimes exchange presents. Hospice caregivers are not allowed to accept anything but cards and food, but at times over the years, I have bought things myself for my patients. For instance, one of my patients once complimented my perfume, so I bought her some. Another time, a patient really wanted a red coat. Her family had purchased a black coat for her and she had been very disappointed that the coat was not red. *Hell*, I thought, *I have a red coat at home and it's like new.* So I gave her the red coat. Truly, it looked better on her than on me. When she put the coat on, she actually twirled around like a model and talked about how a couple of her friends at church would love it. It was nice to see a dying person care so much about how she looked and what her friends thought. Even though she was facing death, she was planning to live. She was in a good place.

The lady with the newly acquired red coat was very poor. I mean, she had nothing. A couple of days later when I arrived for her visit, she directed me to a gift bag on her coffee table. She had bought a fancy bottle of hand sanitizer and a roll of paper towels for me. I cried at this. I cried because I knew that her sacrifice had been greater than mine. She knew I knew that this was the most she could afford. She had apparently put a lot of consideration into this gift because she had watched me constantly using hand sanitizer on my visits and had most likely thought I paid for it myself. The expense, the thought, the sacrifice and the sweetness of this gesture overwhelmed and humbled me.

As I continued making my rounds that Christmas Day, I rolled up to a patient's home and received my welcome hugs just inside the door. My patient chided me for being a bit late, because I had missed their son who had wanted to meet me. I offered my apologies and then they directed me to a big, wrapped-up box in the corner. They explained that it was a gift from their son and he had wanted to give it to me himself. I felt bad about this, but they were very excited and pushed me over in front of the gift. They were clearly anxious to see my reaction when I opened it. As they readied their cell phone cameras, I picked up the present and opened it. As all the cell phones lit up, I could see that the box held a very expensive pair of super-name-brand black boots that go all the way up the legs. Actually they were my size. The cameras continued to flash as they grabbed the boots and helped me get them on.

Everyone was happy and the boots fit perfectly. The family members brought out a mirror from the bedroom and so I could admire the boots, which looked a bit awkward since I had my scrubs on. The family texted their photos to the son whom I had just missed. I have never seen a bunch of people having such a great time giving a gift.

Now, at this point I was thinking that I could not possibly accept these boots. But I also would never insult the family by telling them that on the spot. I understood that this was their way of paying me back for what I love to do. I thought that perhaps I would donate the boots to a good local charity, as I have done in the past, or find someone along my route to give them to. I quietly planned to donate the boots to a worthy charity.

There were other gifts along my route waiting for me on that Christmas Day. Before the holidays, several families had told me they would have presents for me, and I had let them know I would be by on Christmas to open them up. Thus my Christmas consisted of going from home to home to assess my patients and then to open my presents. Only four of us were on duty that day, so I received a few texts and calls from co-workers who were at home with their families. They wanted to let me know they were thinking of me. While I appreciated this, I thought it possible that I was having a better time than some of them who had to put with all the drama and exhaustion that goes with families at Christmas.

The calls and texts began with "I hope you're doing okay out there?" and then launched into an issue with a relative or some other holiday problem. What is always great at Christmastime is the texts that come from the families of my past patients. They don't forget me and I don't forget them. It pumps me up when I see their names on my phone.

At times over the course of a patient's care, I had wondered if their family members really liked me and appreciated what we hospice nurses do. When I get a text, a phone call, a card, or when I stop by for a visit weeks or months later, I realize that they had indeed cared and appreciated all along. We become friends for life.

I also warn them that I may call them from just around the block if I ever get in trouble—and if I do, they need to have their door unlocked.

While my territory is huge, it is good to know that I am welcome back in so many homes for a visit and especially for an emergency.

Another special thing that takes place while I am making my visits during the holidays is the calls from family members, other relatives and friends, and family in the military, jail or prison. The speaker phones go on and the whole family has some great conversations. They always include me and insist that I talk to the loved one calling. I am always really glad to do this. In many cases I feel that I already know the caller because the family has talked about them all the time.

As I drove around that Christmas Day, I heard about all the gifts each person gave and received. I opened presents, visited with the families, met a few new people, and ate until I couldn't eat anymore. After a few more visits, my trunk was full of candy, food and a few presents, and my work shift ended. I headed to my parents' home to see my mom, dad, brother and—if I was not too late—my grandparents. I had told them all not to get me any presents. As I mentioned earlier, I was feeling different this year and just wasn't in the traditional spirit of Christmas. This had been a very stressful year. All the protests and rioting had added to the sadness of the job I do. I had not bought presents. I was not convinced that this once-a-year gift-giving thing was the way to go. Most people just like to give gifts, and certainly children should have presents at Christmastime. They love receiving them. I remember that from being a kid. But I have become more of a "give during the year" person and I really didn't care what people thought about my new philosophy.

It was probably a good thing that I was working that day, because I wasn't doing the normal "Christmas thing." However, I did give myself one present: I was going to my parents' house to get my kitties. I always loved for the kitties to go there because my mom and dad give them so much attention, but I missed them terribly.

When I arrived there, my dad greeted me at the door. My brother was lying on the floor, not moving much since he was sick with the flu. My mom was glued to the TV. She just looked at me and I knew that she hoped that perhaps she would have a few more days with the kitties. There were a lot of opened presents around and food, but no grandparents. I had missed them by half an hour.

Even though I had told my parents not to get me any presents, thank God they did! They gave me a brand new, bright-red set of luggage that matches my car and almost everything else I own, some beautiful clothes, and a single-service coffeemaker that I had always wanted. The coffeemaker was also red. And finally, as they did every year, my grandparents gave me one hundred dollars. I have to say that I always look forward to the money because I always need it for something.

My mom's parents, my grandparents, are two great people. They always tell me how proud they are of me. Who doesn't want to hear that? It means a great deal coming from them. They'd had very little growing up, but had made a wonderful life for themselves. They love each other very much and aren't afraid to tell everyone. It is always a blast to get to see them.

My father's dad passed away a few years back. He was also an amazing person, and I truly miss him. I felt close to him, and as time went on, I came to realize that all of his many grandchildren did, too. Imagine making each one of the twenty-five grandchildren and thirteen children he and my grandmother had feel special and important. That took a lot of effort and caring.

Whenever I see patients leaving special things behind for the family, I think of all the great letters I received from my grandfather. He began writing to me when I started college and kept it up for several years. He had a degree in philosophy, so he offered a wealth of advice and inspirational quotes in the letters. Some of his letters quoted T.S. Eliot's poem, "The Love Song of J. Alfred Prufrock." This was an exceptional poem about a man's journey through life—and all the regrets at the end. This poem helped me to live more fully. My grandfather also sent me audiotapes of him reading the poem. Hearing his precious voice reading his favorite poem is priceless. This treasure inspired me to always encourage those who are passing away to leave meaningful things such as videos and tapes when possible.

I don't see my dad's mom much, but she is a really neat person. Actually, she is quite a bit like me in that she speaks her mind. She is very sharp and interested in everything. She loves nature. There is evidence of this all over her house. She is also very generous in giving to many charities. She worries every day for those who don't have the basics in life.

My father told me that one day, he and my brother were bow hunting for deer way back in the woods near a large lake about forty miles from town. They had been unsuccessful in their quest and had headed back to the truck once it turned dark. As they got to the parking lot, they noticed a car parked there. It was my dad's parents. Everyone was surprised. I tell this story because I think it was interesting that my dad and brother were trying to harvest a deer and my grandparents were there simply to view them. The only thing they had in common was that they both wanted to see deer. They laughed about it.

My parents and I visited for a long time, talking about the kitties, and then it was time to put them in their travel cages and head out. They were hiding under the bed. We wrestled them out and had to force them into the travel cages. My mom gave me last-minute instructions on when she had been giving them their food and treats as well as when they had taken their naps and gone to sleep for the night. It was no different than if they were children. We said our goodbyes and I was off.

My kitties were spoiled with attention from their visit at my parent's house. They were also exhausted when we got home. It was like they were college students home from spring break—they always need to sleep for a couple of days afterwards.

I was finally home and glad to be there. The kitties inspected the house to make sure everything was the same. I cleaned the place up and returned a few phone calls. I have two phones. One is for work and one is personal. I went back and forth between the two phones, returning all the calls and texts. I watched a little TV and played with the kitties and before long it was the midnight hour.

The work phone suddenly rang. I answered and it was Becky, the wife of the patient I'd had dinner with that day. She said she was so sorry for calling me so late, but her husband Ron had taken a turn for the worse. Her husband and the family had shared the common goal of him making it until Christmas. He wasn't going to die that night, but he was getting very close. I talked to her for some time and told her how we would go about addressing the situation. I made the appropriate phone calls and called her back, hoping that our changes to his care plan would give Ron the comfort and relief he needed.

Many men and some women simply do not want to be a burden on the family. Ron was one of those people. He was doing everything he could to not be a bother to the family. Becky, a strong woman with her feet on the ground, knew what he was up to and made sure he got the best care and didn't do anything stupid.

The kitties were finally sleeping when I went over and got that red coffeemaker out of the box and washed it out. It looked wonderful on my counter. I went through the variety of the dozen little packets of coffees and teas that had come with it. I was in the mood for a caramel latte, which I placed in the machine for the morning. It was time for bed for me, too.

As I laid in bed with my kitties thinking about the day, what struck me was that not one word had been spoken the whole day about the protests and rioting. This had been a different and good Christmas, and I felt grateful for that as I drifted off to sleep.

"I hope you hear inside my voice of sorrow
And that it motivates you to make a better tomorrow
This place is cruel, nowhere could be much colder
If we don't change the world will soon be over
Living just enough, just enough for the city"
—*Stevie Wonder, Living for the City*

CHAPTER 31

Missouri: Murder Capital of the U.S.

Not long after Christmas, I took a couple of days off and spent some time scanning through the computer to check out the crimes in my work area. I do this on a regular basis to see if I need to be extra cautious as I make my rounds. As I mentioned before, when there is one shooting in an area, there is often retaliation.

As I was going through the crime statistics, I saw that the year-end numbers were available along with some statewide information. The local newspapers had picked up the information, and the headlines had caught my attention, so I went to the crime statistics for a glance.

I had known that things were bad, but I also wanted to see if all of the Ferguson unrest had been a factor.

After the Ferguson events, it was announced that the St. Louis Police Department would add 160 additional police officers, with a special effort to hire more African Americans. Department leaders also announced that they were going to focus on "hot-spots" in the upcoming year and their approach would be more community based—what they called "neighborhood policing."

What emerged from the numbers provided by the St. Louis Metropolitan Police Department was that in 2014, there had been a 32.5-percent jump in homicides over the previous year. The City of St. Louis had 159 homicides in 2014 and 120 homicides in 2013. The mayor attributed this to the "the Ferguson effect." During 2015, homicides in St. Louis increased to 188, an 18.2 percent increase over 2014.

According to the report, the overall 2014 crime rate had actually dropped by 3.3 percent, but violent crime had increased 5.3 percent. Violent crime increased another 7.8 percent in 2015.

As I examined other related national data, I found some information on the final outcome of the 2012 crime statistics for the State of Missouri and the U.S. As it turns out, that year's statistics are the most recent available. (I wish I had those people's job!)

There were some very sad statistics from the Violence Policy Center in Washington, D.C.

The report showed that African Americans comprise 13 percent of the U.S. population but account for 50 percent of all homicide victims.

In the State of Missouri, the African-American murder rate was 34.98 per 100,000 people. That is twice the national African-American victimization rate for homicides and about seven times the general homicide rate nationwide. This means that, if you live in Missouri and are African American, you are twice as likely to become a homicide victim as compared to other states.

Missouri ranks first in terms of African-American homicide victimization in the United States. Over the past several years, the state has consistently ranked first or second in this crime category. Missouri ranked number one in 2014, 2013, 2012 and 2011.

There were 247 African-American homicide victims in Missouri in 2014. The average age of the victims was 29. Of the homicide victims, 207 were male and 40 were female. Almost 90 percent of the killings were with a gun.

Some research at a website called "Neighborhood Scout" pulled up some additional 2012 crime data. It showed that on a scale of 1 to 100, 100 being the safest, St. Louis gets a '1' on the crime index.

The chance of becoming a 'Violent Crime' victim was 1 in 56 in St. Louis.
The chance of becoming a 'Violent Crime' victim was 1 in 222 in Missouri.
The chance of becoming a 'Property Crime' victim was 1 in 14 in St. Louis.
The chance of becoming a 'Property Crime' victim was 1 in 30 in Missouri.
There were 424 crimes per square mile in St. Louis.

There were 39 crimes per square mile in Missouri.

There were 39.3 crimes per square mile on average in the United States.

The City of Ferguson ranked 6 on a scale of 100 on the crime index.

The chance in Ferguson of becoming a 'Violent Crime' victim was 1 in 265.

The chance in Ferguson of becoming a 'Property Crime' victim was 1 in 19.

There were 190 crimes per square mile in Ferguson.

As it turned out, Ferguson had done much better than the City of St. Louis, at least according to the most recently available national statistics from 2012.

There are specific numbers for the area that I work in and they were all worse than the above numbers. I just wanted to provide you, the reader, with an overview of the crime landscape. As I read the numbers, I thought not only of those who had been murdered, but also of their families who would suffer for the rest of their lives.

In my job, my mission is to make people comfortable while they are dealing with their impending death. My patients and their families know that death is near. They suffer as they get through this process, and those who remain behind suffer again after their loved one is gone. On top of all of the family's agony over the loss of a loved one, those left behind must face daily news of unnecessary killings surrounding them in their communities.

I deal with this agony also. What makes matters worse is that there seem to be no solutions. We talk about it, we cry about it, but we don't ever discuss the "solution on the way." All we can do is let one another know we care—and do a lot of hugging.

CHAPTER 32
The Best Days of My Life

My father recently told me that I am living the best days of my life right now. He went on to say that, most likely, I don't realize it. He also said that he thinks that I will never have a more fulfilling job. Don't get me wrong—my parents wish I had a much safer job.

Early in my hospice work, I would joke about writing down some of the experiences I'd had and perhaps make a TV show. I started telling my friends about what I was doing and mentioned that I needed to do this because the things I saw and experienced as a hospice nurse were so unusual.

I never thought I would write a book, but someone encouraged me and it just happened. My motives for writing the book are not financial. Research indicates that is very difficult to sell any significant number of books, and even harder to make money unless one is famous. I am not famous. There are many nurses and hospice workers doing exactly the same type of work that I do. And there are medical people in foreign countries under almost unthinkable circumstances of poverty and disease. These are the real heroes.

As I began to write this book, I was excited to capture these stories so that I would have them for myself forever. Writing these stories started as something of a diary, but it wasn't long before I found myself wanting to write just because it made me feel better. It was therapy for me. My job can be hard and dangerous, but the people I take care of live in these conditions every day. While this is my job, this is their life.

The combination of the difficulty of the job and the tough environment drags me down from time to time. As I would write, I would cry and laugh, but I always felt better once I finished a chapter. Two of the stories from my earlier years were actually written last, because I just didn't want to relive the experiences. These chapters were especially emotional to write because I deeply miss both of the patients and their families.

When I arrived at the midway point of the book, I stopped writing for a while, and suddenly the Ferguson situation happened. That is what kept me going to the finish line. Juxtaposed against the backdrop of the riots and looting, all of my experiences in caring for dying persons and their loved ones seemed magnified. The patients and families became more outspoken and our conversations more intimate. I became a great listener during this time, and I learned a lot.

What makes me happiest is that by writing these stories, I get to share my experiences with all of the characters I encountered. They were all interesting and unique individuals, and they dealt with their dying or their loved one's journey toward death with grace and even, at times, wonderful humor. The patients' stories are often sad, but the life they had was most often very fulfilling.

Working as a hospice nurse has changed me, especially working in neighborhoods challenged by violence and crime. My basic beliefs have not changed; rather, these experiences have reinforced my convictions and provided me with a deeper motivation to do an even better job.

As I go about my job, sometimes I think about my white friends who will never experience even a little taste of the daily life in these neighborhoods—the life I have gotten a glimpse of by virtue of traveling the final days with a patient and family. I feel blessed to have had the opportunity to do this, and I think it would be wonderful if I could somehow find a way to share my good fortune with them.

From time to time, I am asked to accommodate a medical student to ride along with me on my route. This is actually one of my favorite things to do. I love seeing these young people freak out and try not to show it. At the end of the day, traveling these real-life neighborhoods is a great experience for them, because they get to see where and how some of their future patients live and the resource limitations they may have. Perhaps a few of them may read this book to add to their knowledge base.

In the previous chapters, you read a lot of "praise" for Tia. Almost everyone in each story tells me how much they appreciated me, etc. I originally wrote the book in this way because it made me feel good (don't forget that writing became my therapy), but after reading the book, this tone stood out and seemed that I was bragging about myself. I left it this way just in case I need to read the book for therapy at a future date. I hope you don't mind.

My patients and their families really did say all of the wonderful things to me that are described here. In addition to making myself look good, writing their words down helps me to remember and highlight how appreciative they were. Remembering their gratitude is important. I could not do what I do without all the kind words and hugs. As I fill in for my co-workers, I find that they, too, have similar relationships with their patients. I am not special, but my patients make me feel that way.

I have no idea if these really are, as my dad says, the best days of my life. But I know that my experiences are the most interesting I have had thus far in my life. There may be no other job that could be so challenging but also so fulfilling, at least for me and my capabilities.

Perhaps, then, I really am sharing with you the best days of my life. What made it all possible is hospice. Not that many years ago, hospice was just a concept. While still in its infancy, hospice is becoming a more significant part of the dying process. I look forward to hospice care evolving and growing to compassionately care for all dying patients and their families as they experience one of the worst times of their lives. I wish this most especially for those in the neighborhood I serve.

I may keep a diary as I go forward. I may need the therapy. We may meet again.

About Hospice

I am not an expert on hospice information, but wanted to provide you with some valuable general information from my experience. Refer to the last section for more reliable sources including Medicare, the National Hospice & Palliative Care Organization (NHPCO), and the Hospice Association of America. Phone numbers and website details are included.

The term "hospice" has often been understood as a place—or "building"—where terminally ill persons can go to receive nursing care until they die. Hospice is also a concept of care. When a person is at the end of life and no more can be done to "cure" their condition, they receive hospice care to ease their physical, emotional, social and spiritual needs as they go through life's final journey. The goals of hospice care are to provide support and healing even when "cure" is no longer possible. Hospice care is most often done in the patient's home and includes comfort care, medications for pain management, monitoring for changes in status, and a variety of other services that support the patients and their families. Hospice workers include nurses, nurse practitioners, administrative personnel, doctors, medical directors, social workers, pharmacists, chaplains, counselors, home health aides, volunteers, and security personnel.

Hospice began in the United States in the 1970s. The concept of hospice care resulted from the work of Dame Cicely Saunders from the United Kingdom. In the

U.S., hospice programs are more focused on the patient's psychological issues related to dying, and we have a greater emphasis on people volunteering to support the program.

Hospice is available to all patients of any age who have a terminal prognosis and have been certified by Medicare or other insurance as having less than six months to live. Over a million and a half people have used hospice and it is growing. Over one-third of all patients who are dying currently use the service.

Most hospice patients are in treatment for less than thirty days, but as noted, they can use the services for up to six months and even beyond in some circumstances. Medical providers and volunteers provide services not just to the patient, but also to the entire family, who may need help in caring for the patient's basic needs or who may need counseling support. Hospice is not curative or diagnostic. Normally, treatment just focuses on making the patient more comfortable at the end of life. Some patients do select procedures such as CPR that could prolong their life.

Hospice care costs are covered by programs such as Medicare and other forms of insurance. Care is usually provided in the home but can also take place in nursing homes, hospitals or a hospice facility.

There are four basic levels of care: general inpatient care, continuous care, respite care, and routine home care.

General inpatient care is very involved care for patients in difficult situations. This type of care most often takes place during the last few days of the patients' life and is usually done in a hospice facility, a special section of a hospital, or a nursing home. The patient is usually experiencing severe symptoms that require everyday interventions from the members of the hospice team.

Continuous care is normally done in the patient's home. Continuous care patients are usually in need of extra support from time to time to deal with their severe symptoms. Typically, the patient receives a minimum of eight hours of care per day.

Respite care is for the patient's family. If the family caregiver needs a break, the patient may be transferred from the home to a facility. The facility can be a nursing home, hospital or hospice facility. The patient is then provided the same services that were provided in the home until the caregiver returns. Respite care is available for only five days during each benefit period.

Routine home care is the most widely practiced form of hospice care. The care can take place at home, at an assisted-living facility or at a nursing home. If the care is taking place at a home, the staff provides all the items that would normally be available in a facility, including medical equipment and medications. The hospice provider must also make caregivers available twenty-four hours a day for the patient.

Hospice provides services through a team of professionals for the patient and the patient's family. The team works together toward one goal: They strive to make the patient comfortable and to support the family in coping with the situation.

A hospice team supported by Medicare must meet at least every fourteen days to plan the next fourteen days and must at that time also review the patient's medical condition.

There are usually at least eight members of the hospice team. These include the registered nurses, physician, hospice medical director, volunteers, pharmacist, social worker, counselor and home health aide.

The *nurse* coordinates the patient's care and makes sure that all physical and other symptoms are dealt with. They usually visit the patient at least twice a week but sometimes more often, depending upon the needs of the patient. Sometimes these visits are long and sometimes they are very short. The nurse is trained to handle difficult treatments as needed, including intravenous therapy, wound care or respiratory care. The nurse makes recommendations to the physician for the scope and degree of medications and assists the family and patient by educating them on the dying process and advising them on assistance available to them to cope with all the issues involved.

Most individuals have a primary care physician or a specialty physician. In addition, the hospice program includes a *physician* who oversees all of the patient's medical needs. Hospice physicians are trained in end-of-life care such as pain management. The hospice physician studies the patient's records and sometimes information from the recent hospital stay and then develops a care program for the patient. He or she provides that information to the caretakers, including the nurse. The nurse keeps the physician informed and adjustments are made as needed. Sometimes the physician visits the patient, but not always.

The *hospice medical director* is a physician who usually gives overall support to the clinicians who are providing direct care to the patient and family. At times the medical director may fill in for the hospice physician if needed. The medical director is also responsible to recertify all of the patients when required.

Volunteers are used to a much greater extent in the United States as compared to other countries. They volunteer with the patient by assisting with healthcare, house chores, and errands, and most important, they become companions to the patients and the family. Some volunteers also work in the hospice office, doing whatever is helpful to support the staff.

The *pharmacist* fills prescriptions and continually monitors drug interactions, keeping an eye on the goal for the drug therapy.

The *social workers* are there for the patient's admission to hospice. They take in an overview of the family's situation and when needed, connect them with financial and any other outside resources that might improve the situation and help the patient and family deal with the issues that arise during this difficult time. Social workers also assess the home environment, and if it is not an ideal situation, they may offer options that might benefit the patient and the family.

Counselors can include a spiritual counselor, social worker, chaplain. or others. Counselors are required by the Medicare program. They assist by attempting to fill the spiritual needs of those involved. This may include connecting the family with a requested minister, rabbi, priest, pastor, etc., as their needs may be specific to their religious preferences.

Every patient may not require a *home health aide*. When used, they go to the home as often as every day for a few hours. Some of the services they provide include giving the caretaker a much-needed break or helping the patient with getting out of bed to do various tasks. Sometimes they feed, shower or bathe the patients.

As noted previously, to qualify for hospice care, all patients must be certified that they have a prognosis of less than six months to live. If a patient is on Medicare, the benefits are broken down into two 90-day periods. Once the 180 days expire, the team evaluates the patient to determine whether they still qualify. At that point, if they qualify, then the team evaluates them every sixty days to determine if they are eligible.

At times, some patients are discharged from hospice as a result of safety issues or philosophical differences. Sometimes this occurs when a patient or the family refuses to cooperate with the hospice program. The patient maintains the right to re-enroll in hospice if this situation arises.

In general, if a patient chooses to seek out some form of curative treatment, they would no longer participate in the hospice program. They can, however, stay in the hospice program even if they are hospitalized if they have a different medical issue that is unrelated to the original condition for which they were enrolled in hospice.

If at any time information becomes available that a patient will live beyond six months, they will be released, but the hospice team will provide ample warning so as to not upset the family and the patient any more than is necessary.

Patients are allowed to transfer to different hospice programs if they wish and if they qualify.

Most hospices are paid for by Medicare. About eighty percent of all hospice enrollees are Medicare patients. Medicaid and private insurance companies make up the remainder.

About eighty percent of hospice patients are over sixty-five, but hospice is available to anyone at any age. Some hospice organizations are not set up to handle younger patients. At this time, only around twenty percent of hospice organizations are able to accommodate younger patients. Common conditions for the younger patients who enter hospice are cancer, cerebral palsy, prematurity, trauma, AIDS, congenital disorders, cystic fibrosis, etc.

Additional Information
www.Medicare.gov or phone: 1-800-633-4227
Hospice Association of America, www.nahc.org/haa or phone: 1-202-546-4759
National Hospice & Palliative Care Organization (NHPCO), www.nhpco.org or phone:1-800-646-6460